IN LIMBO:

BREXIT TESTIMONIES FROM
EU CITIZENS IN THE UK

IN LIMBO:
BREXIT TESTIMONIES FROM EU CITIZENS IN THE UK

From an idea by Elena Remigi

Foreword by George Szirtes

Collected and edited by
Elena Remigi, Véronique Martin and Tim Sykes

CONTENTS

FOREWORD

When the EU Referendum on 23 June 2016 was narrowly won by those voting to leave the European Union, a process was set in motion that is still not finished and is unlikely to be finished any time soon. Where it will end up nobody yet knows. Nobody even knew what 'leaving' meant: it seemed to mean whatever anyone at any point said it meant. It took the woman swept to power by it, a woman who had originally supported remaining, Prime Minister Theresa May, to give it its full definition. Brexit, she told us, means Brexit.

But of course it meant something more to those immediately affected by it, those whose lives and futures were suddenly cast in doubt. Chief among those were EU citizens living here and citizens of this country living abroad. What would happen to them? Could they carry on living and working where they had, in many cases for decades, as citizens of a union that would now be broken up. Would those living here be held as 'hostages' against the fates of British people living and working abroad? Would 'Brexit means Brexit' be a sufficient answer to their concerns?

Those concerns had already been raised by the nature and temper of a Leave campaign that overtly encouraged 'British' people to regard all EU nationals as parasites, leeching off systems intended purely for the benefit of native Britons. EU citizens were conflated with immigrants, refugees and potential terrorists from all other places. Foreign simply meant bad. Foreign, to put it in prime ministerial terms, means foreign.

The lives of EU citizens – people from Germany, France, Italy, Spain, Austria, Romania, Hungary and everywhere else – indeed almost all the hospital staff from surgeons down to cleaners that tended me in Papworth in the February of 2016, were all going to be affected. They and others in other jobs, in other places in the UK, were going to be put under the ever increasing pressure of rhetoric from ever more fervent supporters of a campaign in whose eyes they were simply foreign. Having spent much time and energy disparaging 'faceless bureaucrats' in Brussels, leavers could now set the UK's own faceless bureaucrats loose on the spawn of Brussels in this country.

Well, here are some of them speaking for themselves. Reading these testimonies arouses as much admiration as anger and sorrow. So many of them are highly trained professional people with higher degrees and careers who have made valuable contributions to the life of this country, so many others have come here to do honest hard work and made a success of it. Others are here because they married a UK citizen, or are UK citizens who have married an EU national. Others have spent decades here. Some have grown old here after work. They have all contributed.

"I cried at the dentist's today," says one. "Something has broken inside," says another. "I've been stabbed in the back, lied to and lied about," says a third. And so it goes on: "Something in me broke. My heart sank. The hatred is the worst part," one adds. One discovered a valuable peptide that was considered a major breakthrough in the field only to be told she was a burden on the country. Another found a local man blocking their way with his car and shouting abuse at them. "We have done nothing wrong. We are not criminals," pleads another. Some are 'reassured' by being told that they are not the guilty ones and that no harm is going to come to them. We don't mean you. "I go to bed every night crying," one confesses.

Many witness to the warm welcome they received when they first came and how happy they had been here. What has happened since then? What has happened to this country when people who have never done any harm, have lived here for years, and have served the country well are constantly encouraged to 'go home', or insulted, or physically attacked?

What happened? The Brexit campaign happened, relying heavily, as it did, on the suppressed fear and hatred of foreigners, scapegoating them for every possible social ill from the closing of the mines in the eighties and nineties, to the financial crash of 2008 and the general effects of a world-wide globalisation whereby ever bigger money chases ever lower employment costs all over the world. The Leave campaign accused its opponents of using scare stories, but Leave itself had the biggest scare story: eighty-million Turks just raring to overrun the country and queues of Middle East refugees, who were not 'really' refugees but terrorists or freeloaders, waiting to invade us! Never mind the fact that these were not EU nationals: they were foreign and that was enough.

To claim that the results of the Referendum, framed as it was in the blankest possible terms with no particular majority requirement, took the contributors to this book by surprise is vastly to understate the case. It astonished them. The week after the Referendum, I met an elderly French widow at the hospital bus stop who had lived here for thirty years and whose English husband had recently died. She was in tears. She thought she had made friends and got on well with everyone but now, she understood, they never did like her and wanted her gone. Urban Norwich might have been firmly for remaining but Norfolk was solid for leave. Another widow, German-born, of roughly the same age and in the same circumstances, had twice been asked when she was going home. She had lived in Norfolk a good deal longer than those who had asked the question.

One of the surprises awaiting many of the contributors was the demand for CSI, a form of health insurance no one had mentioned or talked about before the question arose. As one contributor notes:

> I do not qualify for permanent residency. This came as a shock to me as I initially thought the application would be a formality. That was until I learned of the infamous CSI (Comprehensive Sickness Insurance) when I wanted to apply for PR.

In all my years as a student or self-sufficient person no one has ever mentioned this requirement to me. Nor have I heard it discussed in the media or otherwise (and I consider myself fairly well informed).

It was necessary to have had it continuously. And if people had taken time out of work, or had spent time abroad, back home, their tasks became much more complicated. Some had had children in Britain, some married British people abroad and brought their children back. Very few knew precisely what to do. Suddenly everything was uncertain and the mood around them was hostile. Those in London had been the happiest. They were living in the most cosmopolitan city in the world and felt part of it. Now they were regarded as interlopers and spongers, burdens to be borne.

The testimonies missing from this book are those of seasonal labourers and very low paid workers: fruit pickers, farm labourers, meat packers, cleaners, terminal carers, and many more who speak only basic English and are exploited by unscrupulous agencies and employers. Looking to write an article about seasonal farm labourers, I rang a major employer to be told: We don't deal with people, we deal with products. Whether these workers – and I have met some – are taking jobs that local people are keen to do and that local employers are keen to pay higher rates for is doubtful. Are local workers keen to live six to a small room in a neglected house? Would they willingly agree to travel in gangs in clapped-out cars provided by the employer and be charged the earth for it? And if the poor foreign workers stopped coming would those businesses survive at all? These testimonies are missing because those who could testify can hardly write English and are terrified of losing their jobs. I met one young Bulgarian couple. He had hopes of working as a tennis coach. They both picked mushrooms for a year – backbreaking work – then moved to a factory where they packed food. There was no competition for their jobs. They still had hopes. They were surviving.

Cheap immigration has been very badly handled in terms of accommodation and distribution. It has been done on the cheap. One perfectly nice man told me he had voted Brexit to stop illegal immigration and illegal workers. The clue, I argued, lay in the term 'illegal'. Illegal immigration was already illegal. It made no difference to him. Some avalanche, a build-up of personal frustrations and the frustrations of others he had only heard about at second hand or read about in the right wing tabloid press, had started in him and it wasn't going to be stopped by a quibble like that. He wasn't overtly xenophobic at all. Indeed, in talking to me he was talking to a foreigner, a refugee in fact, one of Nigel Farage's hundreds of thousands, just a bit whiter. But not all his mates would be exempt from xenophobia. One local taxi driver had moved from King's Lynn because, he said, the Lithuanians had taken over. The proportion of Lithuanians in King's Lynn is 1.1% of the population.

That avalanche is with us now. It is, we are told, 'the will of the people', that is to say of just over half the voters who turned out to vote in the Referendum, that entitles them to roll over everyone else. 'The will of the people' and 'the people of this country', only half of whom had any kind of 'clear will' to leave, is apparently enough to entitle its proponents to set the snow rolling and retire waving innocent hands when that snow turns to an avalanche.

The contributors to this book are the articulate, intelligent, valuable parts of the population on whom the avalanche has descended. They are sick and anxious. Suddenly they feel they are regarded as the enemy. It is no use concerned Leavers assuring them that they'll be all right. It was the fury and vehemence of the Leave campaign that looked to sweep them out. They are not all right.

George Szirtes

INTRODUCTION

In Limbo: Brexit testimonies from EU citizens in the UK is a collection of personal accounts by EU citizens living in Britain that reveals the practical and emotional turmoil they have experienced since the 2016 Referendum on the UK's membership of the EU. Organised by volunteers on a not-for-profit basis, this anthology is a moving and harrowing snapshot of our times with the potential to add real-life urgency to the national debate.

The collection aims to give a voice to a sample of the three million UK residents who are so often treated in our political discourse as a depersonalised mass of 'migrants' – a term which has been used in a derogatory way by the tabloid press and is also incorrect, as European directives on free movement refer to all EU nationals, British people included, as 'citizens': all equal and benefiting from the same rights. In contrast, this anthology reveals them as individuals, whose lives have been interrupted, plunged into limbo, by political events few had anticipated. It portrays them as citizens at home in the European Union, until the rules suddenly changed. In addition, a complementary perspective of British nationals who have settled in other parts of the EU is briefly represented at the end of the collection. Their plight would deserve a book of its own, but we couldn't leave them out of ours as they represent very much our mirror image on the other side of the channel.

The *In Limbo* project originated when Elena Remigi, an Italian interpreter resident in Britain, felt that the numerous EU voices expressing their distress since the Brexit Referendum would have a much more powerful impact if they were gathered together as a collective testimony. She had also realised by then that most people (even politicians) had little understanding of the discrimination and uncertainty Europeans in the UK were facing as a result of the Brexit vote. She decided this collection of testimonies needed to be made available to as wide a readership as possible, including both decision-makers and members of the public alike.

She started a Facebook group in March 2017, called 'Our Brexit Testimonies', with the help of Tim Sykes, a British editor, and Véronique Martin, a French author and academic married to a Brit and a UK resident for thirty years. They were helped in their work by a tireless team of dedicated moderators.

In less than a month, the group had grown to over 1000 members. Its atmosphere was carefully nurtured to create a safe and supportive environment as many had difficult and painful stories to share. The candid testimonies that were gathered between March and April 2017 show the many ways in which real lives have been affected by the outcome of the Referendum, illustrating the practical difficulties and the profound emotional stress that have been imposed on many people by this new political situation.

All the testimonies are shared with the full consent of their writers. Several have preferred to sign with their initials or remain anonymous because of concerns about possible discrimination. Others will never appear in the book, as their writers felt they had too much to lose and were fearful of repercussions. Although they cannot be included, their message is carried by all of us.

Against the odds, the book was created in less than two months as an intensive labour of love and dedication. We have endeavoured to include as many voices as possible. Nevertheless, it has sadly not been feasible to incorporate into the book all of the testimonies. Those that couldn't be included will be published in our associated blog, whose aim is to go on where the book had to stop.

In our approach to editing we wanted to retain as much of the integrity and idiosyncrasies of each testimony as possible. To achieve this goal we have merely corrected typos and removed obvious repetitions or digressions, together with passages that may have compromised the privacy or safety of our contributors. Our aim was to make the texts clearer and tighter, for the benefit of the reader, without losing their essence and individuality.

Reading the powerful texts we had received, we concluded that the emotions depicted in them were rarely clear-cut: like the stages of grief, they were complex, intermingled, messy and prone to changes. Nevertheless, some salient ones did appear and we decided to follow where they would take us. That's when a piece of research undertaken by Dr Helen De Cruz, a member of our team, provided us with the starting point for the book structure. She had asked a sample of 1000 EU citizens in the UK to express how the Brexit Referendum had made them feel, and published her results in the shape of a word cloud, a 'Wordle'. We chose the top five adjectives in the Wordle and they became the scaffolding on which we hung the testimonies: sad, disappointed, worried, angry and betrayed. We then refined that robust but raw structure in an effort to make the stories flow into each other. In the end, although the scaffolding is still holding everything together, it has receded in the background.

This collection is aimed at everybody who is interested in or needs to gain an insight into the true experiences of EU citizens in the UK: members of the public, British family members of EU citizens, journalists and decision-makers in both British and European politics. We hope it will inform but also help fight against discrimination and prejudice by touching hearts and opening minds. People are people wherever they come from, and home is not so much the place where you were born as the place with which you have fallen in love.

During the long hours we spent poring over these compelling human stories, we became aware that a haunting leitmotiv was appearing again and again through the deep uncertainty, the painful state of limbo, experienced by their authors. That powerful leitmotif was the dual question of identity and belonging so essential to us all: who am I and where is home?

The editors

A LITTLE NOTE ABOUT THE COVER

When Article 50 was triggered, Dante's words came to my mind:

"Nel mezzo del cammin di nostra vita
mi ritrovai in una selva oscura
ché la diritta via era perduta"

They translate in English as:

"Midway upon the journey of our life,
I found myself in a forest dark,
For the straightforward pathway had been lost"

(Dante, *Inferno,* Canto I)

These wonderful lines inspired the title of the book but also, later on and quite uncannily, its cover.

I remember sharing these verses with Véronique one night and telling her that I had an image in mind from a copy of *The Divine Comedy,* illustrated by Gustave Doré, in my parent's house. She immediately understood what I was referring to as she was well acquainted with these images. We went on elaborating all night on this and shared dozens of pictures of trees and foggy forests.

When Gareth Harrey decided to help us with the design of the cover, we told him that we wanted to express the situation of limbo people were facing: maybe a person or more in the fog, but we remained very vague. You do not tell an artist what he needs to create.

When he returned with the cover of the book, we simply could not believe it: it was the image both Véronique and I had imagined!

Gareth's cover truly represents our limbo: a place of uncertainty, sadness, confusion, fragility, and many other painful feelings.

Dante's *Inferno* ends with the verse:

> *"E quindi uscimmo a riveder le stelle"*
> "Thence we came forth to rebehold the stars"

> (Dante, *Inferno,* Canto XXXIV)

This is my wish for each one of us. Our limbo is not only about whether we have the right documents to be able to live here or not. There is a psychological limbo too into which we have been plunged. My hope is that we can all "re-behold the stars", as content and settled as we first were before this Referendum.

Elena Remigi

A STORY

A STORY

This is not my story. It is the story of three letters and a postal card written in 1943. They were inside a book given to me by an old Dutch friend. Soon after the war she travelled all over Europe. As she explained: "Mixing with different cultures, even when they are similar, is the only way to prevent hatred and the horrors of war." In 1946 she went to Sweden, to see a Jewish refugee from Auschwitz.

There my friend met an Englishman, she married him and moved to the UK for... good. She would say, over and over again: "This country is good for immigrants and they for this country." She had great faith in the UK's fairness. She gave me the book when she went into a care home. I left the book unopened, because I don't speak Dutch, but one evening I felt very sorry for it, opened it and a white envelope fell on the floor. On it she had written: E.F. The letters were in Dutch, too, but the date intrigued me and I showed them to a Dutch shopkeeper in my town. He read a few lines and burst into tears, crying: "Sorry, I can't! I can't." A few days later he asked me to see them again and translated them. They had been written by EF before going to Westerbork camp and from there to the East. One sentence stayed with me: "The cars are boarded up. Shame, I was hoping to sit by the window." I was haunted by E's words, till it came to me that the letters should go back to Holland.

I offered the letters to Westerbork Memorial Centre, but I could not bring myself to imprison them in an envelope and have them shoved all over the place. It felt disrespectful. I confided in my sister (a midwife who's seen hundreds of 'immigrant' children being born and would die rather than label them in any way). She told me that I had a moral duty to deliver them in person.

And so I did: made an appointment with the director of Westerbork Memorial Centre, booked a flight, train and hotel. Only one specification: seats by the window, all the way to the letters' final destination. No queuing for visas, no cards to classify me as an alien before exiting and entering the UK, and once in Holland, which language but English! Until June 2016, that was the language of liberation, freedom, respect and equality.

This is the EU to me, a means to make amends and give peace to a terrible, past wrong. And Brexit? The answer, as my friend used to say, I leave entirely up to you.

M.T., Italy

PART I

*"I, citizen of Europe, my wings clipped,
my dreams shattered, my freedom chained..."*

I cried at the dentist's today. My dentist is lovely and my teeth are OK. I don't cry easily and it really took me by surprise.

But he asked me kindly how I had been since our last appointment six months ago and I told him what Brexit has meant to me and my husband. After thirty years of life in this country and twenty seven years married to a British citizen, I am not entitled to Permanent Residency. This is because I've never had the Comprehensive Health Insurance (CSI), illegal according to EU standards, which is only now being imposed as a necessity.

I told him about feeling betrayed, let down and abused by the government who did not do the humane and moral thing by us and our families. And who also betrayed and let down the Brits in relationships/marriages with EU citizens as well as the Brits living in the EU, who are now reduced, as we are, to mere bargaining chips.

Then suddenly, in the silence of his room, with his kind and bemused eyes on me, lying on the chair as on a psychiatrist's sofa, I heard my voice break and tears started rolling down my face. I felt mortified but it made me realise the amount of stress and sadness I have been carrying inside for the past eight months. I know that, sadly, my fellow EU citizens here feel exactly the same.

V., France

★★★

I do not remember when my love for Britain began. My mother used to call me 'my English daughter', and joked that on the day that I was born, during the students' protests of May 1968 in Milan, there was an English woman giving birth who shared the same hospital bedroom, so they must have exchanged the two babies.

I suspect I have always been an anglophile. I adored British and Anglo-Saxon literature in general, and during my childhood, spent entire afternoons sitting in an old dusty armchair in my basement facing the garden, immersed in Stevenson, Defoe, Carroll and, as time went on Hardy, Austen, Orwell, and many more. At school, English was my favourite subject, partly because it provided a respite from the rigour of all other subjects. Compared to Latin and Greek, English was easy, fresh, modern.

In my eyes, Britain was a country steeped in history but also open, multicultural, and certainly not as suffocating as the city where I was doing my *liceo,* Pavia. I often dreamt of being able to go and live there one day.

Many years later, when my husband was offered the opportunity to move to Britain for work, I was overjoyed, though I loved my life and work in Ireland. So we moved. Eleven years afterwards, I was completely at home in the UK. I thought a few times of getting a British passport, but kept postponing. After all, there was no need for one.

The Referendum did not come as a complete surprise, because the signs were painfully all there, but it was a big blow nonetheless. After the result, the lack of clarity from the government on our status as EU residents, the choice to use us as 'bargaining capital', spurred me to take a British passport. I studied and passed my Life in the UK test, filled my application, added all the requested documentation, only to realise at the end that they wanted a Permanent Residence number for European Economic Area citizens. I had never heard of PR or the EEA. As far as I was concerned, I was an EU citizen and was permanently living in an EU country. I owned a house, we paid taxes, and never had any need for extra documents. The new regulations, however, required us to have Permanent Residency to apply for a passport. Unlike most wives of British citizens, my husband could at least be my sponsor. He spent hours filling the much dreaded 85-page application. Not only is the form long compared to the European average of two pages, but requires a myriad of documents. Although our son is at university, we had to provide proof of his child benefit, all my husband's salary variations, five years of flights in and out of the UK, and many more documents and bills. Fortunately, he had no gaps in his work and had kept all the documents. After four months, we finally received our three PR cards.

Very relieved, my husband and son started taking the exams requested for citizenship, the language test and the Life in the UK one. We made the decision of spending £1500 per person including everything to obtain our passport. Compared to the average one in the EU which is only a few hundred euros, this was a huge sum to pay, not affordable to everyone, but we did not want to take any risk. If for any reason my husband lost his job or became ill, we could be in trouble. We were already worried enough of his pension matured in three EU countries now that Britain was leaving the EU.

With all the documents ready, I booked an appointment with the National Checking Service. It was expensive, but it would have allowed me to keep my Italian passport rather than sending it to the HO. Before going, I checked and rechecked my documents and was certain to have ticked all the boxes. During the Referendum, the amount of xenophobia displayed had left me drained and worried, so I was a little tense when I arrived there, but the last thing I thought was to be told to return home as I could not provide proof of having lived in the UK for five years. Having PR, owning a house, paying my utility bills, having listed all my flights in and out of the country for five years, having a passport saying that I resided here, and much more was deemed insufficient. There was no proof of my existence in the UK as I was a stay-at-home parent – a Kafkaesque situation which left me humiliated. I was therefore asked to provide everything I could to demonstrate that I lived here. Not an easy task, given that I had moved house three times in the past five years. I spent the following five days frantically gathering testimonies from my neighbour, the priest, friends, and two old teachers of my son; I provided all my bank statements (luckily they were in my name) for the past five years; and had to go from one surgery to the other to ask doctors, dentists and opticians to write letters stating that I used their services. I also gave the Home Office all my medical exams.

When I returned to the NCS (had to pay again) there was a German lady before me who left in tears saying, "This would never happen in Germany, France or even Italy." I knew the feeling. I wish I could have reached her to tell her that I completely understood.

This time my application was accepted. It is now up to the HO to decide my fate.

After this experience, and months of hostility towards EU citizens from the press and politicians, something has broken inside. The bond, the affection I had for this country is still somehow there, but the wound inflicted is still raw. More than feeling betrayed, I am in mourning for a country I admired for its liberal principles and now at risk of losing them.

Elena, Italy

★★★

My recent PR paperwork nightmare forced me to reflect on the fact that for well over half of my life, I have been 'exercising Treaty rights' in two EU countries other than my native one. That is the bureaucratic definition. I, myself, having it always and only seen it as expanding my own bubble, falling in love, travelling, discovering, learning the language, teaching my own, working, leisuring, raising a family, earning, spending, volunteering, experiencing culture, creating, cooking, eating, sharing, cultivating friendships, developing connections, growing roots, uprooting, starting again... perhaps put simply: just living.

My current overwhelming feeling is of sorrow. For myself and all the years spent in this country I now struggle to recognise; for my irreplaceable energy and effort spent in making of this place my home, a place where I now feel alien; sorrow for my family, since I foresee a separation as each will choose a different land where to chase happiness; sorrow for this country and its people, as the so deeply rooted xenophobia is unveiled and a sickening nostalgia for an empire which is no more is revealed.

I, citizen of Europe, my wings clipped, my dreams shattered, my freedom chained, the result of a mad Referendum in which I wasn't allowed a voice. I feel rather lost, I no longer belong.

M.P., Spain

★★★

I moved with my family to Ireland when I was three years old, meaning that English is my first language, even though I am fluent in Italian too. In 2005, when I was eight, we made the move from Cork to Britain and I have lived in the UK ever since. I have always been a great admirer of English culture, and upon arriving here I became fully immersed in it. Within little time, my Irish accent transitioned into RP, and my Italian friends started calling me 'inglesino' (little English boy).

I worked very hard throughout my school life and was blessed enough to win a King's Scholarship at Eton College, after which I was accepted to read Theology at Oxford University, where I am currently in the second year of my degree.

Until Brexit, I never felt the need to obtain a British passport – I thought it was superfluous, given that I was an EU national, and did not feel the need for a piece of paper to confirm something I felt inside. I have no harrowing stories to tell, but since last June I have started to feel as if my Britishness is constantly put under question.

The first time was during the citizenship process, after I had obtained my Permanent Residency card. There is an English language exam which I had previously believed I did not have to take – it was required to prove that I could understand simple questions, know how to use the future tense or be able to talk about a chosen topic, such as school or holidays. Despite having taken 11 GCSEs including English as well as A-Levels, these exams were deemed insufficient. As such, it was still mandatory for me to sit the exam together with The Life in the UK one, as my qualifications did not count unless I already had a degree. Taking the test, where even the examiner apologised for making me come, would have been less of an issue had it not also been for the £150 (+ postage and train ticket money) I had to spend, besides having to waste a whole day during term time.

The second area touches a more personal note. As most young people, I am very active on Twitter and social media. Following Brexit, whenever I have commented on anything political or related to the Referendum, I receive a barrage of insults together with comments along the lines of 'if you don't like it, go back home' or 'you're not British, so who cares'.

I remember conversing with one particular user, who, upon seeing my Twitter profile, gathered that I was Italian; I told him that I was (soon to be) a British citizen and considered myself so. His response was: "My ancestors have been here for millennia, you have been here for ten minutes," and that having a British passport was not sufficient for making me one of "his people". This kind of language is sadly not uncommon, to the extent that you end up getting used to it.

Brexit has brought up two issues. The first is that it has subconsciously validated people who hold these opinions, who now have no inhibitions in making such comments; the second is that this language reminds us that, to some people, regardless of whether we are British citizens or not, our status as EU nationals renders our opinion on the Brexit debate worthless. You begin to feel that your thoughts on this matter are not as valid as those of others, or, worse, that you have no say at all.

My testimony is not about any deep personal grievances, but rather about a sadness and concern towards what I feel Britain may become. What I have always loved so much about this country is its openness, its acceptance, its liberty. Let us hope that this will never disappear and that the deep divisions created in the country I am so happy to call home can be healed.

Andrea Carlo, Italy

★★★

I'm of Danish nationality but grew up in Brussels.

I've been living in the UK for 18 of the last 20 years. Studying at university with years of working in between. I last arrived in 2007 after being offered a job in my previous university department. I went on to study again in between several years of working until I was made redundant while on maternity leave in 2014. I'm now a stay at home parent, after deciding to raise my two children.

I do not qualify for permanent residency. This came as a shock to me as I initially thought the application would be a formality. That was until I learned of the infamous CSI (Comprehensive Sickness Insurance) when I wanted to apply for PR.

In all my years as a student or self-sufficient person no one has ever mentioned this requirement to me. Nor have I heard it discussed in the media or otherwise (and I consider myself fairly well informed). The UK is home to me and my family is here – I might not be able to stay unless the rules about CSI change. Everyone keeps saying, "You'll be fine!" and I really hope that they are right, however I feel unwanted here now, like a second class citizen and so insecure and anxious about the future. I'm a European at heart and the Brexit vote broke my heart.

C.B., Denmark

★★★

I am Italian, and before moving to the UK I lived and worked/studied for a while first in the Netherlands, where I met my Dutch other half, then in Switzerland. In Zurich (German speaking) and in Fribourg (French/German bilingual canton). I moved from Italy with the idea of being away one year and a half. It has been sixteen years, give or take.

When I moved from NL to Switzerland, I got to deal with the paperwork and general pain of working permits, registrations in police offices, and for example to request a reactivation of my phone line, as I had an annual working permit, a permit B, I had to pay a substantial deposit. The year after my other half moved to another city, but he was lucky, because the law had just changed and he had to renew his working permit only every five years, instead of every year like me.

We lived and worked in Switzerland for a while, and then we moved to the UK, the difference in freedom of movement and freedom from paperwork was surprisingly liberating: no registrations to the police or the city hall, no need to get a health insurance (or so we were told), just show your passport and you can work. Great. No more feeling like a second class citizen.

We settled and bought a house. We both work with temporary researcher contracts, but well, everyone around us does. I had a feeling of belonging, a bit like when I was in the Netherlands. I was again in an EU home, a bit of a weird one because out of the Euro and of Schengen, but still an EU home.

Until the crushingly sad morning of the Brexit Referendum, when this feeling of belonging was washed down the drain. I woke up at 4 am and checked the news on the phone: the night before the polls were uncertain, and Farage was declaring "a 48 to 52 result does not mean a done deal", but that was when his side was at 48%. The situation had flipped overnight and he was triumphant. "Yes, it was a done deal. Remainers, you lost, you have to accept that we won!" At work people were shell-shocked, and all rather disbelieving that it really happened. It was Friday and the evening pub session was pretty sad indeed, even if it was a beautiful summer evening.

So well, mine is more of a pre-Brexit testimony, but it is how I felt, and how I feel, and why I do feel like that. Now applying for PR, no intention of applying for citizenship, but with a very bitter taste in my mouth, we bought a house, it's become our home... but now who knows. Sad.

Francesca L. Stefanato, Italy

★★★

From Today, I'm Only Passing Through

I now live in a country, which officially does not have my interests at heart. The government has decided to use my presence in the UK as a means to negotiate a better 'deal'. Let's get this straight: from today I'm a piece of bargaining fodder, not a person made of flesh and bone, not a life entrenched in the tapestry of this country for over thirty-two years.

Yesterday I called this country 'home'. 'Home' is about respect, about belonging, about feeling safe and valued, about being one hundred per cent welcome. But today I don't feel welcome. I've been stabbed in the back, lied to and lied about.

Thanks for asking (no one ever asks), but no, I don't feel safe or valued anymore. I won't be able to call this country 'home' again. It's a broken home and it's breaking my heart.

From today, it's just a place I live in. I'm only passing through.

Roelof Bakker, The Netherlands

★★★

I arrived with my daughter aged three years old in London in 2000. We waited three long years in Paris without my British partner until my job was transferred in London. It took us a few years to feel at home here but finally we did it! My partner and I bought a house together and we spent wonderful moments together until he fell very ill. We were the only ones to look after him and we were scared he would not survive. Twenty years after, we are still living together. The night before the results of the Referendum, I listened to some classical music all night long. I did not want to hear anything about the vote. And at 7 am, I woke up and put the TV on, all I could see was Farage laughing and smiling. Then, I understood that Leave won and I cried so much...

My partner said to me: "You are not going anywhere. I love you and I cannot live without you..." He put a smile on my face even if I am not sure he realised what that Brexit would mean to me. Now a few months have passed and I feel unsafe, sad and angry. I am spending my time waiting for the government to decide for me, without having any say. I cannot bear even to listen to the news. We started to talk about moving to France. Yes, I know France is not always Paradise but that is my country and there, I will be able to fight, to vote and be active about my future... Let's wait and see.

A.R., France

★★★

I have been living in the UK for 11 years now, which is pretty much my whole adult life. I have been a student here, a worker, a business entrepreneur, an activist, a friend, a lover, and a volunteer. I love London because it gave me all these opportunities. I consider London my home. I can hardly imagine living anywhere else. My community is here. Or communities, because I have many different groups of friends. I feel like I belong here. That's why I love London. The people here are from everywhere and they all can feel at home here, and knowing all the various types of people I've met here has made me a better person, I think. And that's one of the main reasons why I cannot imagine living anywhere else. Londoners are from everywhere and they don't have to be British to belong in London.

And yet, after the Brexit Referendum, something in me broke. My heart sank. Until then, I was at home here, and then all of a sudden that day it didn't really feel quite like home anymore... For the first time in many years, I thought I should go...

But where would I go? Since I made London my home, every time I went back to visit my friends and family in Poland, I felt a bit out of place. As if people were looking at me and thinking: 'you're not from around here.' This never happens in London! Every other person here came from somewhere else and yet, or perhaps because of that, we can all feel like proud Londoners. The variety is what makes London. The languages, the cuisines, the cultures...

Or at least it used to feel that way... Everything feels a little bit different now, since the Brexit vote.

So where is my home now? Honestly, I do wonder these days... If I go back, I would feel out of place, I left so many years ago. If I stay, I feel like an intruder.

Many people are scared. Their future has all of a sudden become uncertain, even for those who have lived here for many long years, making a home, working hard, studying, making friends, falling in love with the culture, just like me. Living with uncertainty is likely what awaits us over the period of the next two years while our future is being negotiated by politicians.

But, for me, personally, the hatred is the worst part. I do know that most people did not vote for Brexit because of xenophobia. The post-Referendum panic told me that most peoples' Leave votes were an expression of confusion and frustration with the EU. Nevertheless, the open expressions of racism and xenophobia that followed Brexit have taken a toll on many of us. Some of us don't feel as welcome anymore...

Magda Oljejor, Poland

★★★

A few weeks left and off we go!

In April 1991, I left Grenoble (France) to undertake a student placement in industry and to spend one year at Coventry University to do a Degree (under the Erasmus program). After receiving my BSc (Hons), I had a place at the famous INPG in France but decided to do an MSc in Scotland and a PhD in England instead as I enjoyed living in the UK (especially in the 90's!). I moved around due to my work (Aberdeen, Birmingham, Chester, Coventry, Henley-on-Thames, Liverpool and Swansea) and even left the UK for three years (Cape Town) with a view to strengthening my professional career as a scientist.

26 years on, I am married to a great Scottish woman and have a gorgeous European child. I have recently been refused PR due to my time in Cape Town. We have done a lot of research and it seems for us that our family is very likely better protected in the EU after Brexit. I am saddened to leave this country as I have invested so much (financially, culturally and

socially; I also taught/mentored/tutored over 200 British students in my career) but I am very excited to start a new chapter in my life. Needless to say I feel betrayed by the UK Gov. I am disappointed, hurt, angry, sad but at the same time happy that my son will have a great opportunity to be a 'citizen of the world', able to master three languages. Lastly, the past nine months have been emotionally and physically draining and I look forward to being in a positive and healthy environment.

I came to this country in good faith. I came to this country as a European who studied, worked, integrated, contributed and socialised amongst other Europeans. I came to this country because of its tolerance, its diversity of ethnicity and cuisine, its great music & art, its thriving science & technology and its vibrant multiculturalism. I made the UK my home. I am now a foreigner, a migrant, an immigrant amongst British people. My home has been taken away. The time has come, it is now time to leave.

Professor Bruno G. Pollet, France

★★★

We were always destined to be an international family, myself dual American and naturalised British, my sons Italian and American and my husband Italian. My Italian husband and I met in Italy and decided to move to the UK for a variety of reasons, amongst them, to live in one of the most international and vibrant cities in the world and we were convinced that would never change. Just consider a walk from the East End to the West. From international banks to corners of the town dedicated to Indians, Chinese and countless other nationalities, there seemed to be a place for virtually everyone to make their own space and blend into the crowds that walked amongst the vivid theatre productions, flashiness of the screens in Piccadilly circus and who inhaled the fabulous scents of the restaurants in Brick Lane. London would always be London, so we thought.

I became a naturalised British citizen in 2012, the year London hosted the Olympics. We had been on a high that year, thoroughly proud to be living in London, which flawlessly showed its lovely face to the world. As we watched live gymnastics, we witnessed athletes push their own barriers as they victoriously reached the finish line and we took our kids to the Paralympics to see how even individuals with the most debilitating physical obstacles could perform miracles in the competitions and make history. Anything was possible in London and we felt on top of the world in the best city on earth. As the UK had been our home for the last eight years, getting British citizenship not only seemed like natural progression, but also a privilege to be part of such optimism and diversity.

We had become proud Londoners and were part of the international fabric of which the UK was made.

Our family felt we were welcomed to create our own history here, as we have felt that we belong here. My boys were born here, and despite not having British nationality, have south London accents they acquired in their fabulous state school. They have studied about Guy Fawkes and attended every school bonfire on November 5. Their first home was in Crystal Palace, where they gained an intimate understanding of Crystal Palace Park that would give them a tangible experience when they were later to study Victorian architecture. They have made drawings for the Queen's jubilee and dressed like the Tudors as they have studied English history, which was their own. We have had jobs, engaged in the same social activities as British people and have been totally immersed; this is home.

I went to bed as normal on June 23rd, not in the slightest bit worried that my whole sense of belonging and peace would never be the same and that the country we had called home for so long would so cruelly dismiss us. I, like 48% of us in this country, had voted remain and was falsely deluded into believing everything would be fine. I was awoken in the morning by a text from a good friend telling me to immediately turn on the TV, where I first learned of the horrific result. As I numbly went down the stairs, my ten year old asked me what was wrong and when I told him Britain voted leave, my terrified seven year old asked me if daddy, himself and his brother would be deported. That's a heavy thought for such a small child. What do you say to your seven year old?

You of course, reassure him that daddy's wife and their mummy is a British citizen, that there's no way they would be sent away and why do you make these reassurance? Because you yourself believe that any mother, father, wife, normal citizen who came here to exercise EU treaty rights would never be legally deported.

Reality, sadly, has gradually hit me and I realise that millions of people's lives can indeed be changed because of so many unfair policies regarding EU citizens in particular. I read in horror the stories of stay at home mothers with British children, brilliant scientists and students all not qualifying for permanent residency because they cannot prove certain salaries or five consecutive years work here. The process for permanent residency is even more stringent than it was for myself, as while EU citizens have to prove personal salary, non-EU citizens only have to prove family income. Therefore, my husband could guarantee for my visa but if I had been an EU citizen, he wouldn't have had the right. Why would the laws be so biased against EU citizens? Surely they are the same as me?

My husband decided to apply for permanent residency and for British passports for himself and the children out of fear that citizenship was the only way we could guarantee our rights here. My children do not automatically qualify for British citizenship, because I was not a citizen when they were born. In theory, permanent residency should be enough, but then as my lawyer sister advised me, the government could change any policy at any time in favour of citizens only, so what's next, citizenship-based NHS, education? An initiative by Theresa May (back when she was Home Secretary) to deny illegal immigrants education failed. However, she is Prime Minister now and although we are very much here legally, we worry a bit she may try to pass a similar policy. This is a frightening prospect, as we need to apply for secondary school in October.

So citizenship seemed to give us the most security. Reluctantly, my husband has taken the Life in the UK test and taken an English test even though he has lived here since 2004, speaks perfect English and holds a professional qualification obtained in English in the UK. We also paid an extortionate £3000 and he has taken a day off so we can get fingerprints and pictures for their biometric passports. We are waiting now.

Sadly, the citizenship ceremony will not be the same celebration that I had, when we had lived in the London that survived 7/7 and hosted an Olympics that made us proud to be Londoners. We have discovered a darker side that we never knew was so prevalent in the UK, one that scorns immigration and welcomes divisiveness. I have come to realise this divided country has been created by self-serving politicians who have been feeding their citizens meals of propaganda with a *Daily Mail* dessert. I realise, with a heavy heart, that the country, possibly heading into a recession, will never be the land of opportunity where Erasmus and free trade is possible and part of the greatest period of peace Europe has seen. People are shocked to hear that yes indeed, my boys and husband are at risk because they figure 'good people like us would be sorted', not realising how Brexit has affected their neighbours, colleagues and friends and how Britain will never be the same.

Holly and Roberto Demartini, USA/UK/Italy

★★★

I am half British, half French. I was born and brought up in France and came here as a teenager. I spent a lot of my childhood visiting my English family. I have now lived in the UK for 49 years; I have had a great life here. I am married, have three grown up children and wonderful friends.

I am just about to retire, after working all my working life, contributing to this society in public service.

June 23rd threw my world into disarray, I was not prepared for the impact this result has had on me. I am dismayed at the awfulness of the divisions that have come as a result of this government hurtling towards a cliff edge, I cannot understand it.

I applied to have a British passport, spent three months having various documents translated at high cost as it has to be done by approved translators. After a few months, a few translations costing £50 odd pounds each, to and fro communications and mixed messages, I was told I was not entitled to a British passport as I was born in a year that means my mother cannot pass on her nationality to me. Why this could not have been told to me at the start of the process before I spent over £300?

All this time I have felt European with my heritage both English and French.

What now? I do not know. I feel quite bereft and certainly not at home.

Brigitte Morton, France

★★★

Today I am feeling numb and a tad depressed.

I have been floating in and out of this for nine months now and am finding it harder to cope as time passes. I had somehow hoped that triggering

Article 50 today would have taken the mounting pressure off my system, but it isn't happening, not today...

I am uncertain about my future, unable to build my herb business, unable to apply for a Lottery grant for my dementia project, my whole future here hangs in the balance as EU citizens are being used as bargaining chips.

We are not being told anything. Goal posts keep being moved. Brexit is a string of lies. We cannot trust Theresa May and this government. An increasingly hostile environment is being created.

As it stands at the moment, after 22 years of working and paying taxes here, I have no entitlement to settlement (leave to remain) post Brexit, because I don't earn enough before tax as a self-employed person.

This makes me anxious. This makes me sad. This also makes me angry, sometimes.

I came to this country 22 years ago to do a job. They recruited me for no one else could do in this country: interpreter and translator. I have since moved on, become a successful international art dealer and set up an arts charity and arts centre and sculpture garden. Three years ago, when my business partner retired and I was too ill to continue the business on my own, I changed direction once again and am setting up a business growing medicinal plants to produce and sell herbal antibiotics. I have also set up print making workshops for people living with dementia and their carers. These are a huge success.

In order to be able to continue with these projects, I need to know I will still be able to live and work here post Brexit, in 2019. I am applying for a big Lottery grant for one, and an EU grant for the other project, as well as needing to borrow money, so EVERYTHING is currently in limbo. Grants are for three years, my break-even point is five years from startup but EVERYTHING IS IN LIMBO!

I fluctuate from happily working on building my garden and my business and looking to applying for more grants for the dementia project to wanting to chuck it all in and put my property on the market and leave. I had it valued, best get out while it is still worth more than the remaining mortgage perhaps?

But where do I go? I am Dutch, but I made the Welsh Borders my home. When I arrived here, I felt instantly at home, welcome, wanted, appreciated. I love it here! I bought my little house with the view to settle and stay here. I am part of the community to which I actively contribute. I want to keep doing that! FOREVER!

Not until some power crazed politician felt it a good career move to promise a Referendum on EU membership and leave it to the largely uneducated masses who are in no position to decide on such a thing... It sucks!

Do I hang in? Do I take control, sell up, and leave? Leave EVERYTHING I love and worked for? I am sad. Sad for this country. Sad for my fellow EU citizens. Sad for those 48.2% of Brits who didn't want to leave the UK. And even sadder for those who brought this right royal mess upon us all!

Hanneke van der Werf, The Netherlands

★★★

I came to the UK a few years ago as a 'highly skilled migrant worker'. I had to obtain a visa waiver as at that time the labour market had not been open to Romanians. I was headhunted; I was not looking for this job and actually had never considered working in the UK before.

I worked around the world and depending on the context, I assumed different identities: in south east Asia I was a 'Western woman'; in the US I was a 'European'; but I became distinctly 'eastern European' in the UK.

I wore my 'label' with pride because I thought it meant somebody who had grown up under a very repressive regime (where being caught listening to the 'Voice of America' or owning a 'forbidden' book landed you in jail) and, through his or her hard work, could live up to the expectations of 'being European'... That was until recently.

Somebody kindly explained to me that the 'invasion' of 'third world Europeans' from Romania and Bulgaria into the UK was the last straw. That's what did it.

What have I brought to the UK for my 'invasion'? All my savings, which I sunk in a massively overpriced London flat; ten hour work days; my knowledge and skills developed without any contribution from the UK; a farewell to my pension, and a pay cut from my previous job. But I did think it was worth it because I had the chance to be a part of the most progressive, educated and diverse of societies.

When I look around me, at my friends and colleagues, I still think it is worth being here. Unlike some of the soul crushing stories I've read, I have not experienced any discriminatory treatment, except for the one comment I've mentioned above. On the contrary, I don't think I've been hugged more by my British colleagues and friends than since the Referendum. They are just as flabbergasted as I am. And they don't want to live in a closed minded intolerant society either.

I had the chance of leaving, but this is home now. And I am here for better and worse. I feel I cannot leave my best friends just when they need me most.

I think we, the Europeans, East and West, share a dream with the 48% of Brits that is worth fighting for.

Nicoleta, Romania

★★★

Where home lies

I come from a place that is not my home
To a place that is not my home.
As choices were taken – but not for me
Or made by me – choices made in the fast time,
In a thought's flicker – in the dry, hard walk
Of not making choices for the future of others.
Choices for the now, for the right now,
My life was taken and I was deposited right there.

Vincent Berquez, France/UK

PART II

"I have done nothing wrong,
we have done nothing wrong."

'Where words fail, music speaks' (Hans Christian Andersen). Each musical performance is story-telling, I keep saying to my choirs. And with reference to Andersen's words: singing especially is often about expressing that which can't be expressed in words, which touches audiences. This quotation has always inspired me in my work as a conductor. Although Austrian-born and native of Vienna, I settled in Bangor in late 2013 to work on my PhD in Musicology at Bangor University.

Today, I am spreading my passion for music-making between diverse rural communities in North Wales: in Flintshire, the Isle of Anglesey, in Llanfairfechan, Wrexham and in Bangor, where I am teaching conducting at Bangor University, and work with the university's own Symphony Orchestra.

This is now at risk due to the UK's exit from the European Union. On the eve of the fateful Referendum, I had a concert with the traditional Welsh male choir, Côr y Traeth. We received standing ovations that night, not least as I was introduced as an Austrian musician. Three days later, the final episode of Penelope Keith's popular Channel 4 series, In Her Majesty's Service, was aired, which prominently involved Côr y Traeth and myself. Incidentally, at the time of shooting in mid-May 2016 at the picturesque Caernarfon Castle, I had frequently engaged in heated debates with friends and members of the public about the Brexit Referendum, which once ended with the call for putting me "on a boat back home on 24 June."

Despite having lived in the UK for about ten years spread over two decades – I first had lived in the UK between 1997 and 2006 with periods of work in the Midlands, as well as the studies at University of York and the Royal Holloway– I do not qualify for PR status. And at this stage, the CSI cover issue prevents a possible application in 2019. I still keep making music, as words fail me to describe how I feel at this point in life.

Matthias Wurz, Austria

★★★

I am one of the highly skilled individuals that the UK wants to or should want to keep. After an Ivy League education in the US, I could have chosen to stay in almost any country in the world. England, however, won my heart when I decided to go to the University of Oxford for my PhD. We tend to complain when new arrivals don't integrate in British society, but we forget to think about what happens when they do. Naturalisation, the process of embracing the culture and integrating (not the bureaucratic process for citizenship), worked for me. I soon fell in love with the society's openness and tolerance, the industry's meritocracy, the people's pragmatism, and the loveliness of the English countryside.

Now, almost ten years later, I am a valued employee of a major bank. I look back at the country that was, the country that is, and the country that will be. This is not the country that my English teacher, Glenis, talked about since when I was four. The country's government, my government, 'values my contribution' but has at the same time turned hostile on me and the ones I love. In a game of high-stakes poker, they say I am invaluable to them, but they refuse to guarantee my right to stay. It is difficult to describe how much this hurts. Sometimes languages are not strong enough to describe feelings: How does an orphan child describe the pain of losing its parents? How does a resident describe the pain of being pushed away by his government? I feel terribly let down, like a lemon squeezed for its juice and then conveniently discarded.

The PR portion of my citizenship application was rejected last year. I was expected to have CSI during my student years, a requirement that was never advertised back then, even the Home Office failing to list it as a requirement. Ironically enough, I did have private health insurance, but the assessing officer exercised their discretion to rule the cover inadequate. The term 'comprehensive' is ill defined for health insurance; without clear guidance from the Home Office, it would have been impossible to obtain the right cover.

I have always held a Panglossian view of the world. Both my fiancée and I are highly skilled, highly mobile, and highly employable individuals. If the UK drives us away, we will build another life elsewhere. The hurt, however, from the pound of flesh the government is extracting, from the friends that silently watch while this takes place, and from society's unwillingness to discuss anything Brexit... That hurt will always be there.

Philip, Greece

★★★

I first came here and moved to Scotland nearly 22 years ago after marrying my husband who was in the Armed Forces. We moved around the country both in Scotland and England for years and years. I got friends in my various workplaces around the country. I am still in touch with many of my Scottish colleagues from over 16 years ago. I visited Scotland in 2015 and met loads of them.

The whole story would be too long to tell, but my husband left in 2014. A few weeks later I found out I was seriously ill. I had to have emergency surgery while in Finland, followed by six months of chemo when back home in England. Yes, this is my home. I never thought things would change so much that I saw some people thinking it's not my right to call it home.

I am still officially married, as I haven't received any paperwork from my other half. What I did find out after the Brexit vote is, that even though I'm still married, that doesn't count for PR, as we live apart. I can only apply because of my long stay. Luckily I have been here very long and my current job alone covers more than the required five years. But I'm still not sure what is accepted as proof if I am missing some of the paperwork. I don't trust the process, even though I can get proof from my employer (a department of the UK government).

I cannot afford the citizenship process, as my pay from the government that issues it is so low that it would cost more than my monthly wage.

I have been told by a Brexit voter that "it's not you we are talking about". I had to say that the word immigrant definitely is about me! Just like a black person is black and a gay person is gay, an immigrant is an immigrant and you can't just be anti-immigrant and tell one of them: "I don't mean you!"

Most of the Brexit voters I know are much wealthier than I am. They don't have to suffer so much for the rise in energy prices due to the fall of the pound, or the rising inflation overall. I have not heard of how this country will get better with 'taking back control'.

I have felt really bad after the vote, even though I have never myself suffered any abuse. The continuing stories in newspapers talking about migrants this and migrants that, talking only about who is a 'useful migrant' who can stay or come here. Nothing about the fact that people come and stay for various reasons, like marrying someone British. I left a good job when I came here and made this country my home. I could say, like in the old TV series, that I am not just a number. We are all humans.

M.L., Finland

★★★

I decided to stay in Britain after coming to attend university, first as an undergraduate and then to do a PhD in neuroscience. I got a job as a research scientist and I fell in love with a British woman. In 2013, we got married in Edinburgh where her father was born. I wore their family tartan to our wedding.

I had always put off applying for British citizenship for various reasons but when the EU Referendum was announced I knew I wanted to do it. I had lived here so long, had contributed to the economy, and integrated into society. Yet I was not even given a voice in the most momentous votes of our generation. No more taxation without representation. I got together the required documents, passed the citizenship test, and was ready to go through with it – except that I then learned I needed to get a Permanent Residence card first. This was in March 2016. The requirement for a PR card had only been introduced six months earlier. You can imagine how I cursed my tardiness!

You have probably already heard of the infuriating 85-page PR application and its requirements for additional documentation. To make a long story short, my PR application was rejected because I didn't include my passport. The letter from the Home Office also told me to 'make arrangements to leave' the UK. My case has since then been covered repeatedly by the news media, such as the Guardian and Independent. Lots of foreign news organisations also wanted to interview me about it.

Unfortunately, all this news coverage tends to present a quite distorted picture. As I said, I applied for the PR card in March 2016. I was rejected in June, a week before the Referendum. All the news articles saying I 'anxiously' sought to secure my right to stay after Brexit are wrong. At the time nobody – not even Nigel Farage – thought Brexit would actually happen. I applied for PR because I wanted to become a British citizen and that was because I believed this country was my home.

However, for the past year I have felt increasingly unwelcome here. Don't get me wrong, most of the British people I talk to are just as horrified by what is happening. Many even apologised to me and said how ashamed they are of their country. For a German this feels weird – we are so used to always being the ones apologising for things our country did that aren't our fault... But the hostility and red tape of the Home Office, the utter lack of compassion and respect by the Brexiteers running this government, and the general rhetoric about 'Europe' made me realise that

I don't really belong here. I am also pragmatic. The pound is low and the economy will inevitably suffer from the consequences of Brexit. Access to research funds and the ability to hire talented scientists for my lab will be greatly diminished. And politically, the next few years in this country will be a complete mess.

I therefore decided to leave. This place is no longer my home. Perhaps it never really was. It is no secret that on the whole the British have always been sceptical of the EU. This was partly driven by the distorted and offensive tabloid press but I believe there is also a latent xenophobic streak in the national psyche here. Some people, including Remainers, just can't seem to get over the idea that people can be at home in a country where they weren't born. Whenever I say that I will leave, they automatically assume that I want to 'move home'. I have no great desire to return to Germany after I spent most of my adult life in Britain. Where do you think my home is? I admit there is a part of me that will always feel connected to Lake Constance where I was born. But I believe that home is where you take it. I'm ready for a new home in a country that treats its immigrants with respect and where I can be happy again.

Dr Sam Schwarzkopf, Germany

★★★

I'm a pharmacist that's been here since 2002, got married to a wonderful woman (non-EEA), had a little boy and bought a house. Everything was going well, we had finally settled and everything was going great for us... until the Referendum.

The day after, when picking my son up from school the atmosphere was very icy. Before then we'd had a good relationship with the other parents. There were comments and children were listening to them. Then, of course, there were the same problems at work: a so-called colleague brought a cake in to celebrate that we were leaving and another one asked me when I was going to be deported. I consider myself an educated person and would have NEVER said that to anybody, not even as banter. Also, as my accent is not 100% British, I get all sorts of situations when working, with people asking me when I'm leaving, etc. I know that this is common nowadays, unfortunately, but I just wanted to share it.

Mariano R.G., Spain

★★★

I was 14 when I first arrived in London, I took part in a summer school programme and stayed with a hosting family. I will never forget how welcoming and exciting it felt to be here, and how odd the host family thought I was for asking at what time would the tube come and never quite figuring out which way to look before stepping off the pavement! I absolutely loved the month I spent here and was determined that I'll find a way to live here at some point in my life. After finishing university in Hungary with flying colours, I applied for a PhD scholarship at Cancer Research UK/UCL in 2010 and got accepted (there were 1250 applicant for 25 places). I was over the moon, and although I started out with very little money and had to live in an overcrowded accommodation for three months (12 people in a six-bed house, I shared a room with a stranger), I quickly managed to get a nice double bedroom in a house share so my boyfriend could move to London too.

We got married the next summer, and seeing that my PhD project was going very well, we decided to try for a baby. We moved to a one-bed flat – our first flat together! Our first son, Oliver, was born in 2013 at UCLH. I only took four months off, which was paid in full by CRUK, then returned to finish the project and get my PhD. My work focused on tetanus, a deadly disease, still claiming the lives of 70,000 people each year (two people will die from it in the 30 minutes I'm writing this testimony). There's a vaccine but no cure and it is simply not affordable to most of the developing world to vaccinate the entire population. I found that a peptide could prevent mice from getting tetanus, this was considered a major breakthrough in the field. Science Magazine, one of the most prestigious journals in the world, published it in 2014. After the PhD I became a postdoctoral research associate at King's College London and soon received a four year fellowship from the Wellcome Trust. We welcomed our second son, Milan, to the world in 2016, and after nine months' maternity leave, I went back to work, trying to figure out what common cause might lie behind epilepsy, autism and schizophrenia.

I applied for PR before the Referendum, and ignored the requirement for a Comprehensive Sickness Insurance for students, since I didn't see those years between 2010-2014 as student years – I was working hard to find a cure for a disease! Plus nobody has ever heard of CSI, and I couldn't get any advice on what to do about it. After an anxious six month wait (we found out that the Leavers won in the meantime) I got the refusal letter, simply saying that unless I can prove that I wouldn't have been a burden to society had I fallen ill between 2010-2014, these years cannot be seen as me exercising treaty rights and being a resident in the United Kingdom. A 'burden'?! I discovered a cure for a disease during these years!

I felt devastated and got a sense of not belonging anywhere, as if I was homeless...

My second son, Milan is a British citizen. He was born in five months. before the Referendum, I applied for his passport based on me being a resident in the UK in the five years before his birth and we got his passport straight away. There was no need for CSI for this.

Here we are today, two Hungarians working full time (my husband is a highly respected swimming teacher), one Hungarian and one British little boy and we are not sure what to do. My funding is primarily British, so financially speaking it should be safe to carry on, but there are no guarantees that the conditions of the contracts for EU nationals won't change after Brexit. The Institute I work in receives most of its funding from EU sources, the head is Spanish and the workplace is a complete mixture of people from all places on Earth – this is a great blessing of being a scientist! We have 15 people in our lab, and 12 different nationalities. Ever since I started my PhD, I felt like the world was my oyster; the atmosphere that London offered was open, liberal and intelligent. Maybe it was a bubble, waiting to burst, but I enjoyed every minute I could be inside it. I would like my children to grow up in a place that empowers them and reinforces the idea that no matter where you come from, if you think well and work hard, you will succeed. I thought I found that place here in London, however, it disappeared – but I'm sure I won't give up until I find a place like that again.

Dr Kinga Laszlone Bercsenyi, Hungary

★★★

I was made redundant in France and since I was in my late forties and France sadly is very ageist, I decided to come to another country that always had the reputation of tolerance, fairness and open mindedness. So I came here in 2010, and my daughter joined me in the adventure. She was 20 and out of university.

We came here with all my savings, a tiny flat rented in Kilburn central London and an immense optimism and faith in this country. We found a job less than one month after, in the same shop, and all was great. I moved to Kent in 2013. After one year of struggle, I managed to find a job as bilingual customer service executive, but the salary was really low. Once I paid my rent in a shared house and my train fares, I was left with less than £200 to live, but I didn't complain as I was in the country I chose and loved and people were so nice.

Then the June Referendum happened. I could not believe the results, even if I was not surprised as Kent voted massively out, and I had been told to "return to Frogland, bitch" but still it was a shock!

Ever since I lost my job, I have sent numerous and hundreds of CV, had a few interviews but nothing. I have received a letter from the Job Centre saying I had lost the right to remain here and they would stop my benefits (sadly I had to claim). I was left destitute as I had no money at all, because with the low salary, I could not make any savings.

I contacted my MP, who wrote a letter to the DWP, and I am now thankfully back in the system, but that was such a fright to know that at any moment I can receive such a letter and that I am now under scrutiny. I am making a herculean effort to find a job but to no avail.

To settle in England I have made so many sacrifices, and now I am not welcome, I feel I have done all that for nothing, it breaks my heart so much that I have sunk into depression, I sleep with sleeping pills, I've become a hermit. I want to return to France but for that too I would need money and I don't have an income at the moment so I am stuck. I feel like a fly trapped behind a window, I am losing hope and I am so sad.

A part of me still loves this country, but another sadly no longer does. I no longer can look at people in the positive way I used to.

Voilà.

Murielle Stentzel, France

★★★

I came to the UK out of love and to build a startup.

My love decided to come here to work with Stem Cells for her PhD and I followed also because the startup ecosystem back home (Lisbon) was still too immature. So she arrived 2011 and I late 2012 after a few months working in the Netherlands.

The initial startup didn't work and I went to work for a German multinational managing their software contracts all over the world. End 2014 I tried again and opened with a partner a data science consultancy company. Immediately we won a European Data Science Award, 50k in financing and even offices in London. We became a tech startup. Our project was at the heart of one of Europe's major problems: we developed AI software that would allow to pinpoint and track suspicious boat activities down in the Med. From very small boats to everything else.

Then that project went bust for several reasons (some due to the way it's difficult to make a consortium of very different partners to work together) and we proposed a second alternative: a way to use online data to match jobseekers with companies, thus fuelling an emergent European job market. In between we did others too: for instance for a client in Australia, helping social care people identify children at risk of being molested and another one here for the government. This one was essentially to obtain insights from all the social and health care data in various platforms.

The biggest knowledge we delivered was a deep correlation between government cuts and a drop in standards, by region, local area, almost to the street level. This tool would then be made available to the public and local authorities. Unfortunately, this outcome was badly received and we got the order to shut it down since it was 'too political'. Nevertheless we are just software developers; it's not our job to hide the truth within numbers, but to provide our customers the tools to make the best use possible of them. We got back to our jobs tool and delivered a prototype that generated a lot of interest from big names in the sector. We then went on discussing with several possible European partners a project to further its scope and tech. We were discussing with a university in Poland, a French company, a Portuguese one, a UK one, and were pretty much in line for about further two million in funding.

Then Brexit came and it all collapsed. I can now say the company is closing in the UK and we are moving abroad to try again. Some people asked me why don't you stay? For us, I think it's a matter of principle. Yes, funding plays a role obviously but we can find it elsewhere. What we can't find elsewhere is something like a consortium where three or four companies from all over Europe pull together a project and share resources and people and markets to make it work. Even if I was offered five million tomorrow, it would be impossible to achieve the same level of resources, expertise and previously made work, besides the market. It would be incredibly more expensive. But as for the 'principle': it doesn't make any sense for us to build a tool that allows the creation of a European job market, from outside or from a country that doesn't see immigration, 'brains' as something crucial for countries and innovation. You see, despite all that is said about immigration, only 1% of people actually leave their countries to work elsewhere, where in the USA it's 10%. We want to change this. So we've decided to leave.

On a personal level, I also don't agree with all the latent racism we've seen in the past few months. For us, the U.K. was the land of knowledge. We now already see how the brain drain is gonna affect this country, deeply.

Now the UK is on the way to become something else, something we don't see ourselves be a part of. I feel a deep sense of detachment from this country and every time I read a headline or what the government says, this notion is reinforced. Since in AI we have something called reinforced learning, it seems impossible not to learn that I'm no longer wanted here. I sincerely wish you all well and hope things work out for the ones that want to stay, as well for the ones like me who for whatever reason have decided to leave. I was very happy here for a while and the UK is a beautiful country, with some very smart people.

Antonio, Portugal

★★★

I met my husband in 2004 during a British-German trade union summer camp in the tiny village of Tolpuddle in Dorset. I attended the camp as part of a student research team evaluating intercultural education programmes, whereas he was nominated by his Trade Union as participant from Yorkshire and the Humber.

After the camp hubby and I stayed in touch via letters, emails and phone calls for eighteen months until he visited me in Germany for the first time in early 2006. I returned the visit in spring 2006 and spent a week in the North of England for the first time where I fell in love with the people and countryside.

In autumn 2006 I returned to the UK to work as a foreign language assistant on a temporary teacher exchange programme after finishing my degree in Germany. I got a placement in Doncaster close to my current home in Huddersfield, where my husband has lived most of his life – what a coincidence. It meant we could meet regularly and get even closer over the course of my stay.

I started to toy with the idea of staying in the UK for good and successfully applied to train as a teacher, which kick started the seemingly inevitable journey to where I am at now or, more precisely, where we as a family with two children stand now.

My husband and I built our family life on free movement, secure in the knowledge that living in each other's countries would always be possible without any bureaucratic hurdles. Choosing the UK as our place of residence made sense because I already spoke English and was at the beginning of my career whilst my husband had a permanent job, a mortgage and no German language skills. I quickly felt at home and part of this society, never realising that a considerable part of the native UK population thought otherwise.

We have had two children early on in our relationship and in my career because not everything in life is always straightforward and perfectly plannable. We welcomed our children into the world knowing that there would be plenty of time left for my career. Of course I did ask myself questions often, questions revolving around the topics of economic independence and work life balance, and practical questions concerning childcare and the associated costs; ordinary issues affecting most UK families.

The fateful day of the Referendum changed everything. Suddenly we became an EU/UK family which, like many others, is in limbo, divided by other people (aka the UK government and Home Office) due to our differing nationalities. I am one of the countless EU parents who are unable to obtain residency papers due the fact that I have decided to look after my children as a homemaker twice during the last decade. Unknowingly we have all broken a very little publicised rule, the requirement to have CSI when exercising treaty rights as a self-sufficient person. CSI is needed in order to reside lawfully in the UK in such circumstances and to build up the five continuous years of residency required to obtain permanent residency and proceed to citizenship (if one wishes to do so).

The next shock was discovering that there are no other ways for EU nationals to obtain a PR permit – even the strongest family ties count for nothing at all. My marriage, my children, my life during the last decade in this country aren't good enough reasons to be granted any security now. I was ready to naturalise before the Referendum, but all doors are currently closed to me and whether any door will open again remains uncertain.

The very decisions we have made in the past in the belief that it was the right thing for our family have turned out to be decisions that are now threatening our future. I'm lacking adequate words to describe how that feels.

Nina Andrea Roberts, Germany

★★★

I grew up in a multicultural family, speaking Dutch and English (background Dutch/ Cuban/ Polish / Ukrainian). We lived in Surrey as children, but also moved around the world a fair amount. My parents loved the UK and we visited often when not living here. I also went to British schools when not in the UK.

I went to medical school in the Netherlands, but spent nine months doing research in Oxford, which is when I fell in love with the UK as an adult. After I finished my training in the Netherlands I moved to the UK to do my specialist training for 11 years. This was a wonderful time. I moved back to the Netherlands for work, but after 13 years realised my heart, social life and (so I thought) future were in the UK...

Brexit happened whilst I planned the move...we still went ahead and moved back eight months ago. As I have been abroad for 13 years I have no right to PR (I never bothered before as there was no need). I love living in London and being 'back'. I work hard and contribute significantly to the NHS. I will stay if I can, but I feel that part of the amazing tolerance and multiculturalism of the UK has been tarnished by this insane vote and this destructive government.

Dr S. Lesnik-Oberstein, The Netherlands

★★★

Letter to my British Friends on the Day You Refused me Protection after Brexit

Let's share a cup of tea together before you kick me out...

Dear British Friends,

I love you. I've lived with you for a long time. I know your culture. I've read your books and watched your shows. I've worked in your companies, I've been squashed in the tube with you and I've walked in the British countryside with you.

We have so much in common. We are friends. We stand up for human rights and we certainly stand up for each other. I know you can stand up for our rights. I know you can fight. I remember your stories of protests against the poll tax. I remember how we marched together against the Iraq war. We didn't win then. The British government went to war. But we continued to protest. We made the case against what we thought was immoral and a violation of human rights. In the end, we were proved right. (Other EU countries refused to participate in that war, they were also proved right.)

And now? You see, after the Brexit Referendum, when 48% of you voted to remain, I expected a lot of protests and I of course expected a strong political opposition, both in and out of parliament. After all, half of the population needed to be represented. After all, almost half of you knew what this meant and would therefore fight it to the last. But nothing happened. There were no big protests. There was no resistance in parliament. No opposition. To someone who didn't know what the percentages in the Referendum were, it must have looked as if 95% of Britons voted to leave. If you looked at parliament. So I was disappointed but I also couldn't understand it.

So I talked to you, my British friends. I've known you for a long, long time. We share so much. European civilisation. Cultural references. Thoughts, ideas, dreams. We don't always agree. Of course not. But we do agree on basic human rights, on ethics, on how to treat others and how to create a fair society.

We still do have all this in common. We do. With tears in my eyes, I say that. But when I ask you, hand on heart, look into my eyes, with all that we have in common, and considering I came to the UK a long time ago, in good faith, considering that I worked here, and in fact I worked in the one industry that accounts for up to 70% of GDP in the UK, which most of you don't, when I ask you: why didn't you do anything to stop Brexit, what is your answer to me?

'There's nothing I can do'. But when I dig deeper, there's another answer: 'It's a pity but I don't think it will affect me. Much.'

But, I say, first of all I believe it will affect you, quite a lot, but, I say, look at me, your friend. Whatever happens to me, Brexit without protection will hugely affect me. I will lose my rights to live here as your equal. Rights that I still have today. Rights that will be taken away from me from one day to the next, in two years' time. I had no right to vote on this. I had no say in my fate. So I need you, my British friend, to stand up for me. Will you?

And, when you don't, when you try to change the subject, when you talk about other human rights issues and also how you can't do anything, really. Yes you did protest in the past about other things but this is different... I realise that what you are saying is this: 'I am safe'. That's what it comes down to. You, my British friend, feel that you are safe. Nobody is going to disenfranchise you. Nobody is going to take your rights away from one day to the next. Well, actually, some of your rights will be taken away as well but obviously, as I find out now, you don't care about those rights, not a lot, as I see now.

You are safe. Nobody is going to deport you. You are safe. But I am not. I will lose my rights. I have done nothing wrong. I came here in good faith, exercising my rights of a 'secondary citizenship' in all EU countries. But now, without a vote in it, without a right to appeal and, more importantly, without even an attempt at protection from you, my British friend, I will lose those rights and I may well be deported.

Deported. Do you know what that means? The police can knock my door in at dawn. I can be handcuffed and forced onto a bus or a train. And then onto a ferry. How would you feel if that happened to you? If that was a potential threat to you? If you had done nothing wrong? How would you feel if your lifelong friends, who did have a vote in this, knew that this would happen to you and did nothing? How would you feel if you were about to lose everything and your British friends abandoned you? How, my friends, even if you are willing to passively support Brexit which in my opinion will bring ruin and disaster to your country and my country as it still is today, even if you are willing to make that Brexit happen by not stopping it, how can you refuse me your protection?

Yes, I am emotional. I have every right to be. And not even you can take that right away from me.

Nyla Nox, Europe

★★★

I don't remember when I fell in love with England. But I remember I was very keen on the English language – I read Agatha Christie books, Jane Austen and the Bronte sisters books and so on. I used to buy tea and bacon at the M&S store in Lyon. Through my school, I had penfriends in England, Ireland and Canada. Because I was let down by France (I could not get a job after my final studies), England gave me the opportunity to work as a French assistant and housemistress in a very peaceful seaside town in East Sussex.

I loved this boarding school because I met girls from all around the world. They were from very wealthy backgrounds but, in the school, we were all equal. The colour of your skin, your accent, your religion – we were all celebrating our differences and respected each other. They were my family and the staff made me feel so welcome that I felt straight away accepted and the best moments of my young adult life, I spent with them.

I stayed there for two years, embracing the English culture and language until I met my husband. That was 32 years ago. I got married, had children, moved to the north of England, made friends, enjoyed the Yorkshire countryside, and then it all changed in June 2016. I am not welcome anymore. The language used to describe us is not the language I have learnt since I was a child. I feel hurt and betrayed. I am completely heartbroken because I have always seen the good in people, and, for me, to see the hatred is like a dagger in my heart. I have done nothing wrong, we have done nothing wrong. We are not criminals.

P. R., France

★★★

I am writing as the wife of a German man and as a daughter of refugees from Nazi Germany. My parents, one Jewish and both political, were always very grateful to Britain for taking them in – although only a few were allowed in. We always had good links with, and friends in, Germany but I felt British and saw it as more tolerant than Germany – until recently. A few years ago, I decided to apply for German nationality – reclaiming my lost one as I saw it, but also because I imagined Brexit as a possibility and saw how welcoming they have been now to refugees unlike Britain.

I am a child psychiatrist and have always worked in the NHS and with refugees. I felt secure and that I belonged. Since June, I no longer feel as secure though nothing tangible has changed for me. Somehow, it has brought into the foreground a feeling that I have always had – that belonging here was just temporary and that we may become refugees again. I saw it as a phenomenon to do with being a 'second generation of refugees' person and certainly had not expected it to be to do with my German husband who is from a family mostly rooted in Germany.

Our children see themselves as European or global citizens, travelling and living all over the world. Our daughter has fallen in love with a German woman who has come to work in the NHS in the UK. Brexit makes her position less certain even though Britain now faces a huge shortage of doctors in the NHS. I don't know what this means for their future. How come Germany now seems the country of refuge and tolerance?

Dr Julia Nelki, UK, parents refugees from Germany (married to Michael Göpfert)

★★★

I came in 1977 to learn English and join the NHS in order to get a good training as a psychiatrist. I passed my language and psychiatric exams and then trained as a child psychiatrist. I started specialising in parents with mental health problems, which later led to the successful publication of a series of books.

Somehow emotionally I probably was a 'refugee' from the unspoken and 'secret' Nazi past in my family and all around me in Germany. On arrival in the UK I struggled with the all-pervasive presence of Nazi insignia on books and in some cheap magazines that seemed on display at every station. Every time there was a foreign policy issue or crisis I had an acute sense of anti-German feelings welling up in the way people started talking e.g. on the radio. But there was always a muted sense of acceptance and tolerance albeit slightly patronising at times to balance this out.

With Brexit I have a sense that this has happened again and it feels much more permanent and final. I have now had a family in Merseyside, three children with British passports, and a wife who comes from London. I am now retired on an NHS pension. Despite all this it feels much more fundamental and suddenly I do not have a sense of having the right to be here and that also seems more final. Even not knowing whether to go for permanent residency in this country when other people's is refused with a notice to start preparing to leave the country feels very different, i.e. something has changed fundamentally. I have put all my adult years and working life into this country, contributed significantly over the years and am in a situation where I might have to fill in a very long form, with exact details of when I left and re-entered the country (which I will not be able to account for). I thought I would live my life out in this country because my family are here. What will happen next?

Michael Göpfert, Germany (married to Julia Nelki)

★★★

I was born in Portugal, one of the last fascist regimes whose motto was 'Proudly Alone' and the last European empire. A son of the African/Portuguese colonial war, I belong to the first generation to be born free after the carnation revolution of 75. Descendant from black African slaves and white colonialists, I grew up with the values of humanism and my bedtime stories were about that fascinating period where people stood up for what was right even if means the end of their status quo.

I learned about the fact that one couldn't own a lighter, couldn't marry a nurse and a flight attendant. Women weren't allowed to leave the country without the male's permission and to kiss in public was considered an exhibitionist moral attack and if caught one would be taken to the nearest police station where you would be fined and have your head shaved. They would even measure the height of children's skirts, every day at school gates, so that the knees would appear covered. Also visited the secret state police torture chambers where my family quite often would go for a 'Friday night' party because public political debate was forbidden.

Today we are amongst the most welcoming, easy-going and peaceful countries in the world and my 6ft Homo-Sapiens build was carved with the notion that I have the obligation to go out there and know the world, to experience different ways of living, to absorb and to teach, to speak and to listen but never to be silent towards unfairness and conservationism of past outdated values... and that brings me to Brexit and beautiful and sunny Scotland.

After working with a Nepalese circus, composed of former child traffic victims (Circus Kathmandu) I moved to Scotland with the intention of going back to study, this time Archaeology. Instantly fell in love with Scotland and the Scottish/British people living up here and I should state that I never came across any kind of xenophobic episodes and the majority of the people I know are against this Brexit nonsense but, at the same time, it's so strange for me this lack of public outcry, this amorphous acceptance that we are giving up humanistic values in favour of blue passports, easy speeches and outdated nationalism nonsense.

I learn to laugh with Benny Hill. Blackadder and Monty Python built my love for sarcasm and I will never forget that in Britain a French gendarme will always say 'Good moaning'. That's the Britain I know, that's the Britain I love and that's the Britain I fight for every day.

I do not have any strings attached to Britain other than love. My profession (lighting engineer in the music industry) allows me flexibility of movement and it's fairly easy for me to settle in different places, been doing it for many years, but I decided not to apply for a resident permit and I'm not leaving the country either. I will wait for the deportation document, if the future follows this idiotic path of isolationism from one of the most important achievements of mankind – 28different countries, people, cultures, sensibilities and knowledge living together for 60 years, taking turns to do the dishes and clean the carpet liquor spilling from last night's party after we nearly destroyed ourselves 70 years ago. I will use it to create awareness, to shout out that this shouldn't happen in 2017 and to tell our kids that the future is a blank page waiting for them to write poetry, that their future is a virgin canvas and it's up to them to choose the colours, and that the heat of tolerance can bend iron...

Take care, my fellow sisters and brothers, and a special greeting to my fellow Brits living in Portugal, who I know are very disturbed with this unnecessary and backward decision.

Eliseu, Portugal

★★★

My partner Stefano and I, both Italians resident in Oxford and both having PR cards, were victims of a hate crime just few days after the Referendum.

It was an early Saturday morning and we were in our left hand drive car (UK number plate) driving on a side road in Oxford when a middle age white man blocked our way with his car at the junction with another road. He started shouting against us in a very aggressive way telling us to go back to our country while keeping blocking our way. My partner wanted to go out of the car to talk to the angry men but I stopped him as I was afraid of the consequences.

This surreal situation lasted for nearly five minutes (it was quite early in the morning and not many cars around) until he had to move because of another car approaching behind him. I called the police straight away and I have to say they were very supportive as they called us at home three or four times apologising for not being able to come and see us for taking a full statement. In the end we were invited to go and talk to the police at our earliest best opportunity which we did on the following Monday.

The police officer was very kind and supportive and he took all the notes and a description of the men and his car. Unfortunately we were not able to get the car registration number and this is the reason why the police could not get hold of him, which is a shame.

What to say? We have been living in Oxford for almost ten years and we never had any problem but now I can see and feel that things have changed and, given the likely bitter tone of the negotiations, it could potentially go worse and worse. We have changed our mind about the fact of keeping on living in England for long time... to us it is not the same place it was before and we will be moving at the earliest best opportunity.

Lucia de Ferrariis, Italy

★★★

I do by now sound like a local (and I don't have any reason to speak German in public usually) and nobody knows I'm 'a foreigner' in daily life, so I have not got any experience of any xenophobic comments directed at myself, as most of my eastern European friends who still have strong accents have.

Still, I am sick of comments like "YOU are fine, it's those (insert nationality of your choice) we don't want..." Usually none of the ones making those comments have ever lived abroad, most have their family nearby, none appreciate what it takes to move to another country, learn another language, leave family and friends behind, for whatever reason, for love, to give your kids a better life, to get a better education, to see the world, to challenge yourself. It isn't something you do lightly, and most people build a new life where they move to. Your home is where you make it. To then be told Britain 'should look after our own' and to be excluded from 'our own' after paying tax and therefore funding a British pensioner, the NHS, a British child to go to school, help funding the UK university I got my degree from and working for the NHS for most of my time here etc. is more than a kick in the teeth. Not being able to vote in the Referendum was another one. (I still maintain if UK citizens who'd been living outside the country for more than 15 years could not vote the only fair thing would have been for EU citizens living in the UK for over 15 years to be able to... fair play was supposed to be the most British thing.) My MP never even bothered to reply to my questions about why he chose to vote against protecting EU citizens' rights, not even by standard reply.

I'll be fine 'legally', I can easily get PR and I can afford citizenship if I need to. I have no way of moving anywhere WITH my partner (too old, no qualifications or language skills), and I do not want to separate after 16 years. I find it very hard to be surrounded by friends who voted for Brexit, who think one European nationality is better than another, who think everyone but me is coming here to sponge of the state, who still think 'everything's going to be alright' even after seeing where the government is steering this, and at the same time are outraged at the idea of Scotland leaving the UK. I wish I'd live in a more open-minded area and had more pro-EU friends. I feel like an island on an island. Suddenly I am a foreigner, and have no right to have an opinion on Brexit, even though I'd be one of the people it'd affect the most. To me the EU is all about trying to work together and trying to get along, and to me this country always was about working together and getting along too. I don't know where this hatred for the EU comes from – well, I do, but I didn't realise how deeply embedded it was in the average Brit I guess. I hate nationalism and cheap slogans, and Brexit has brought out the worst in so many people. It makes me wonder what else they hide, what other opinions they have I never knew about for 16 years...

On the morning of the Referendum result (even though in my heart I knew the outcome already after the most passionate thing I heard anyone around me say about voting to Remain was "I'm voting remain. Though I might still change my mind tomorrow..."), hearing the triumphant Farage declaring he'd "Won the war!" I cried, something broke inside me and I wonder how long it will take for it to be put back together, or if indeed it can be repaired for good. I will fight all the way to keep my idea of freedom and future, though really I'd rather curl up into a ball and wake up when all the current nastiness has subsided. I seriously feel like it's not an unthinkable step for the UK public supporting a war with a European country in their quest to be the ones who are right (and the stupid comment on Gibraltar recently has not helped that feeling).

Where's my home country gone, and why is it suddenly not my home country anymore according to a lot of people?

Natascha Schmidt, Germany

★★★

I came to the UK in 2008. For the first three years, I was 'only' a student on an MSc and then a PhD program. In 2011, I started teaching at my university, and found a great postdoctoral job in a matter of weeks after getting my PhD. I was planning to build an academic career in the UK, and my research, networking and CV-building activities were all tailored towards that purpose.

When Brexit started to become a reality, I looked into PR and realised to my dismay that despite the fact I had worked since 2011, I was not eligible. This was because in 2015 I took several months off work to finish my thesis and look for a postdoc job. During this time, I lived off savings and did not sign up with the Jobcentre, on the one hand because I did not want any benefits, and on the other, because everyone knows that academic positions are NEVER advertised through the Jobcentre. My thinking was therefore, to use the jobcentre would have been a waste of public resources, and I wanted to be a 'good immigrant' and sort myself out.

It emerged, however, that actively looking for work does not make one a 'jobseeker' – one is only classed as such if registered with the Jobcentre.

I had therefore fallen into the 'self-sufficient' category, and since I was unaware of the CSI requirement, I had effectively not been exercising any treaty rights for this period of time. What I get for being a 'good immigrant' is therefore the fact that I am not eligible for PR and won't be until 2020.

As is normal for early career researchers, I am looking at another couple of years of working fixed-term contracts before I hopefully find a permanent job. Without PR, this means that every time a contract ends, I now not only face financial trouble, but a very real possibility that I might not be re-hired at all because I cannot prove my right to work. Moreover, if I have to move for a job, I will not be able to prove to a prospective landlord that I have a right to rent. In other words, when my current contract ends in early 2018, I will face not just 'normal' job market insecurity, but a cliff-edge scenario that may leave me homeless and unemployable.

For this (and many other) reasons I have decided to quit the UK and return home. I might be unemployed there too, but at least I have a flat back home and the dole is actually liveable. I don't know if I will be able to work in my field there, but at least I will survive, which makes me luckier than many others. The UK loses a future taxpayer and a not-so-bad brain, but it would seem that brains have gone out of fashion here anyway.

Ann Bonny, Austria

★★★

Before Lithuania became part of the EU, I lived for a while in the UK on a temporary visa, fell in love with the country and left with tears of sadness in my eyes. Ten years later after graduating from two universities with Master's degree the nostalgia for UK won the constant inner conflict and I made a decision that I couldn't live anymore without the place I felt I belonged to.

As a mother of three, I gave up job as a public servant and came back to UK in 2010, a few years after Lithuania joined the EU. Started from hospitality jobs as a cleaner, later I had been promoted, thought I was doing good, but my husband decided to become a bigger man then he already was and to show us all our place. Suddenly police, social services, court hearings, victim support services, psychologists etc. interrupted our seemingly happy family life and me with three children had to flee to safety losing home, possessions and job. Life became like in a sad drama movie, but thanks to support of friends, UK citizens and all support programs of this country, I managed to get back on my feet.

Finally I got into university got my law degree, found pro bono opportunity at a High Street law firm, started to work for a mentally disabled children charity by giving free legal initial advice, working as a part time sales assistant for a retailer, working as a part time sole trader by helping few small companies with their legal issues as a PA, but I am not making enough sometimes to pay bills and yeah I am struggling financially, that is way I feel threatened by a Brexit. But at least we were feeling safe, protected by the state up until the Referendum when everything changed and fear came back to our lives.

I hate feeling a victim, I don't want to be a victim and I decided to fight back by enrolling to another university just to get one more master's degree in law. Why? Because only with through knowledge we can fight the darkness, arrogance, anger, hatred in people. Only knowledge opens minds, doors, and closes angry mouths.

Despite the fact that we all have gone through the pain of being picked on because we suddenly became foreigners, we suddenly became strangers, I still love this country, traditions and values. The electorate can't be blamed for everything because they have been deceived by politics, their minds have been played with and twisted by a few angry men with charisma.

O.M., Lithuania

★★★

I started a new life in Scotland aged 27. I had finished first my apprenticeship as a cabinetmaker and then a course in furniture design at college. My first serious relationship had ended and I felt this was a good moment, in 1997, to find a new life.

I worked as a self-employed cabinetmaker at first, I could not find employment as a female in my profession. I loved it.

I had a relationship with a colleague and I became a mother in December 1998. The relationship did not last and I faced raising my son on my own with no support from anyone. I was extremely poor and lonely. At first I started by working on a market with my son on my back, doing hairwraps and later also selling hippy clothing for someone else. I enjoyed the community of festival markets.

In January 2001 I opened my own fair trade shop with £5000 my mother gave me from the inheritance of my grandmother, who had died recently. Two years later, I opened my second shop specialising in silver jewellery. I had up to four mums from various countries working part time for me and I felt so happy to be part of a strong female community. In 2011 I thought about going back to Germany, but my community was too valuable for me to lose.

However, since Brexit I have become very distressed and needed a lot of support from my friends, and I discovered I essentially do not have any real friends anymore and am now unsure if I ever did. One person I asked for help in the shop, and on and off employee who I have known since our boys started primary school together told me I should stop reading so much doomsday press. Another, whom I have known equally long, an Australian national married to a Scot and in possession of ILR told me nothing in life was certain, that was just how it was, the government could take her ILR away just as they were taking my rights away, that was just how life was.

Yet another, who had voted for Brexit for 'socialist reasons' asked me not to speak about it as to not wreck our friendship, but believes health tourism is something that needs to be dealt with. This person I would have also called a friend, but now I wonder if she was just friendly to me because I was her boss for 12 years... There is so much superficiality in so many people. I am a kind of 'you get what you see person' and had seriously not realised how much is just small talk and grinning and bearing in so many social relationships. How very German of me.

I am unsure if I can get Permanent Residency. I did not pay myself very much during lean times and I received working families tax credit as a single mum for years, although I always send way more VAT to the government than I got back in benefits. Accountancy advice made me pay myself in ways that some of my income is not classed as earned. The loss of my community is what keeps me up at night, though. There have been many nights when I saw the sun rise because I could not sleep.

My son, who has just turned 18, feels Scottish, so I have applied for citizenship for him on the strength of his Scottish father to whom I was never married. I have been waiting since November, I was asked to pay again but managed to prove I had paid already. After four months I requested his passport back, I got all documents back with a note that I needed to be ready to supply them again once they were processing his application. So we cannot make any plans for him when he finishes his Highers in the summer. He had hoped to go to Berlin, but cannot risk leaving to study in Germany until we know he has British citizenship as he may not be able to return. He has already missed a Christmas trip and cannot go to a family re-union in May as we need to be ready to re-send his documents at the drop of a hat.

I love Scotland, I am settled and I felt like I was part of this country. Now everything is tinged by worry, insecurity and sadness, I cannot help feeling like that, although I am fully aware how much more welcoming it is then some parts of England. A few people have expressed I should not be here or should not have an opinion on politics in my host country, but it's not threatening to me. It is more the lack of emotional support from my closest community that breaks my heart.

Uta Rosenbrock, Germany

★★★

I came to the UK 39 years ago. I came to join my partner who was living here. At first I felt very homesick. Thirty-nine years ago, all shops locked their doors at 5:30pm. There were no coffee bars where one could go for a cup of proper coffee and chat. To my great surprise, January 1st was a working day! I longed to go back to Venice, but I adapted.

We married, bought a house and raised two daughters. I enlarged my group of friends and, as my Italian friends went back home one by one, I acquired new English friends. Finally, I came to think of England as my home. I felt integrated and at ease. Then the Referendum came. 39 years are almost a lifetime.

Now I feel a foreigner again, and more than that, I feel unwelcome. But how can I go back to Italy? I do not feel I belong there anymore than I belong here. I've become a foreigner in my own country as well as here. Besides, my daughters are British and have their life and work here and I want to stay near to them.

I do not know what I am going to do. I shall wait and see.

Marina Bellin, Italy

★★★

Brexit itself for me is only the final straw really, having seen years of changes – and not for the better – in England.

Roll back to the 80s: I first came to England during holidays. Aged 17 my feet first touch British soil in Dover and instantly I felt like I had arrived HOME, where I belonged. Au-pair a year after I completed school, back to Germany, five years later, summer 1992 back to London. The idea was 'a few years, see how it goes, then travel the world....' Well, travelled a little bit, mostly backwards and forwards to Germany for brief family visits.

Having grown up and been school educated during the 70s and into mid 80s in Germany I always felt I was brought up to feel somewhat guilty and ashamed for being German. In England and especially in London that weight fell off my shoulders. Where else (in Europe anyway) could you live under one roof with flatmates not just from England but also Jamaica, Nigeria and Australia? Fantastic years those were. I worked all across London, taught German in adult education as well as in the City. From the Bank of England to Lehman Brothers (yuck!) – Goldman Sachs was probably the worst. But hey ho, this was in the 90s, before we knew they were about to wreck the Western World and beyond.

My son was born late 90s. Planned and much wanted. We never lived with his EU father. Motherhood changes one's outlook on life and south London was not really where I wanted my son to grow up. I dropped my hours to work part time not prepared to leave a baby or even toddler in some nursery setting to be looked after by others from 8am to 6pm. Compromises. At this point I contemplated moving back to Germany (family support, better standards of living etc.) but no, no, no, this was not going to happen. Absent father threw a spanner into those works, rushed to court and no way would he let me take my son to live abroad! At the time the courts were so much in favour to grant parental responsibilities to unmarried fathers, if you asked me not always for the benefit of the child.

So instead of moving back to Germany I took my by then three year-old son and we moved to the Kent coast, beautiful Broadstairs. Initially we knew no one. I left my work, my friends, everything in London to start all over again building a new life. What followed were not easy but mostly happy years I will cherish. Just looking at the sea each day is heaven. New friends, dog, allotment; years do fly by.

We all know 'the world as we knew it' changed after 9/11 and certainly after the financial cock up 2008. Deprivation all around, living standards (yes I know, not just in the UK) have been going down and down and down. For quite some time I had decided I would leave the UK once son flew the nest. Along comes summer 2016! None of us here will forget how we felt on that horrible day in June. In addition only two days earlier my lovely landlady suddenly died and we were given marching orders. Over the years in Kent I had done childminding as well as teaching, tutoring and hosting foreign language students. So not only were we losing our home, I was also losing most of my income.

My son, at that point about to start a two-year BTEC course and I had some discussions on what to do…. Who for starters would take us as tenants with two dogs? Rents and bills near £1000/month for properties of inadequate standards, short tenancy thus no security and where you need written permission to put a nail in a wall. Forget that!

House clearance followed, furniture sold, lots given away, first boxes are abroad, old documents burnt on the allotment, so up in flames my remote chance to apply for PR – not that I'd wanted that anyway. Thankfully a dear friend took me and the dogs in.

My son initially (summer 2016) talked about applying for British citizenship, moved into student house share. Within months he said he would go to Germany once he finishes his course. However, by now both of us had enough.

He is doing exceptionally well in the course he enjoys I'd like to add. He is entitled to financial support but we have been going round in circles since September. Not a penny. He is classed as 'Person from Abroad', regardless of having spent all his life here. There is no need whatsoever to insult children or should I say young adults.

We will visit my parents next month and will find out what options there are in Germany for him. He needs and wants to continue his education. At 18 he has got plenty of time, we are not too worried. It's a good age to be at.

For a long time I have known that I do not want to grow old in England, which once upon a time I loved so much. We will move on. Having myself moved location several times and having seen so many close friends go I do know it is always hardest for the close ones who stay behind. For oneself it's a new start.

We often have choices in life; carry on what we do, take a turn to the left or right? Worst thing is not to move at all. Right now is a tough time, just treading water, but hopefully not for too much longer.

Brexit is speeding up mine and certainly my son's move off the island of no hope. I expect some sadness but mainly a sense of relief will fall upon me once we board the Calais ferry with our last bits for the last time. Neither of us feel 'German' or 'British' – we are Europeans and want to remain that way. The tolerant multicultural country that England was is no more.

I will leave Kent shutting another door behind me; sadly this is not quite how I had wanted it to happen. I feel for my dear British friends who have to stick it out. I worry about their children's futures. I am deeply saddened but I don't want to stay any longer in a country where probably 80% of the people who voted Leave only did so out of utter ignorance and having failed to inform themselves upfront about such an important issue. Strangely since June I have lost my acquired British sense of humour too.

I arrived in the UK with two bags, I shall leave with one car load, my son and the two dogs and a head full of many happy as well as sad memories and an immeasurable amount of life experience.

I have already said my goodbye to Britain, only physically still here, waiting… New beginnings, they won't be easy but will be worth it. I am just not sure yet how I will feel watching the stunning white cliffs of Dover disappear on the horizon when we leave home.

Tina and Felix, Germany

* Tina, born in 1966 in Germany, lived in the UK 1986-87 and permanently since 1992; Felix, 1998 born and lived his whole life in the UK. Both are hoping to leave England by July 2017.

★★★

I arrived in the UK in 2006. In 2014, I applied for PR for myself and my family members including my husband and my three sons. Our application included more than 3 kg of documentations, yet after three weeks it was refused on the grounds that we had not supplied the relevant documents, and because in the Home Office view, my husband did not finish one year of continuous employment for the first year.

We appealed to the First Tier Tribunal giving the exact same evidence. Appeal was raised on the grounds that the decision was not in accordance with the law, as regulation 6 of schedule 4 of The Immigration (EEA) regulation 2006 was not taken into account.

We won the appeal, but the Home Office appealed to the Upper Tribunal claiming an error of law. Appeal was allowed by the First Tier Tribunal Judge. After two hearings and analysis of documentations, the Upper Tribunal Judge decided that the First Tier Tribunal Judge made an error of law but had reached the correct decision. So eventually the Home Office Appeal was refused and a month later all five of us received PR. Two months later, after receiving my PR, I applied for British Citizenship which I received on 3 April 2017. The whole process took me more than three years and was a dreadful time for me and my family.

In my work as a welfare advisor, I witness injustice as to PR and the status of Europeans in UK with regards to benefits. Vulnerable people are put at risk of poverty due to benefits being taken from them without any warnings. It's hard to express how I feel reading those stories from my customers, who do not know where to turn to for help and guidance. It's sad and I feel powerless. But I cannot change it or stop it. I can only fight for them.

M., Poland

★★★

We are a mixed family – I am German, my partner is Chinese with a Finnish passport, and our four year old daughter is a Manchester-born mixed race girl with a Finnish passport. When my partner and I met in Helsinki, we spent a few years living there, a little while in China and some months in Estonia before we decided to settle in Britain.

Why? Because this was the most multi-cultural, open minded, welcoming place in Europe. We did not want to live in cold Finland (although that might have been the better option in hindsight), and we did not feel well in not so tolerant and status quo oriented Germany. The UK was a comparably rough place, high crime, high in poverty, poor on benefits and social security and not very well-paying when it came to jobs. But it was welcoming, people were great and I still feel happy whenever I come back from Germany and the first person says "Cheers, mate" to me in Manchester Airport for a small favour. People here are friendly to kids, and everything is so much more easy going. Not to speak of the tax man. I do like HMRC, and I know that this attracts a lot of irritated reactions from English people who just don't know what they have.

But now what has happened? Over the course of the last seven years we have been living here, we have seen the nation's bigots, racists and nationalist right wingers become empowered. They now dominate any political discussion, and the Brexit vote has created a toxic atmosphere of spite, hate and dissent.

I am disappointed we have been targeted again and again, sometimes by actual thugs and bullies (often online, rarely in real life), more often by the ignorance and lack of education of ma people claiming they "want to take their country back". If it wasn't for our friends and our work here (I am a martial arts teacher and run my own school in Manchester), and if we hadn't just bought our own place, we would be packing already.

We are looking into Scotland, we are contemplating Canada, where quite a few of our friends are headed to. Most likely it will be Rotterdam for us. This is a sad situation. The tension, the hostility and the xenophobia are much worse here now than they ever were in Germany during my lifetime.

Britain is right now losing the best among the immigrants living in the country. Those who are highly educated and can easily find work elsewhere are going already. It is sheer idiocy.

By the way, I have been told again and again that I am "not an immigrant, but an ex-pat", coming from a wealthy country. THIS is an insult in itself.

As a side note: We run a little publishing business in Manchester, too. Leaving the EU, the costs of trade will go up too much. If a book carries a profit of £2, we can't afford bank fees of £20 for a single remittance, for example. We are currently exploring the Estonian e-citizenship to take the company there.

Just another small example for how business unfriendly this whole Brexit nonsense is.

Heero Miketta, Germany

★★★

I came to Britain in 1997 to do a research in the field of history and ethnology. While here I met my British husband, stayed and we got married. I always felt the need to be in an open minded society, where I felt welcome. Did not know how wrong I was nearly 20 years later. We have two lovely children with dual citizenship and both travel on an Austrian passport like myself. I worked before we had children and after my first child was born. Then I studied and after my second child I stayed at home, as we felt my husband earned enough to support us all. Like so many mothers I started to become self-employed to supplement our income – which turned out is not enough to qualify for PR when I looked into gaining it after the Brexit vote. We always regard both of our incomes as ours and find the talk of 'can my British partner be my sponsor' quite frankly annoying and somehow implies that such person in need of a sponsor is less worthy of being an accepted member of the British society. There is plenty of that type of rhetoric floating about in the media that encourages us to think that way. You earn, you are in; you don't, you are not worthy of Permanent Residency, let alone be called a valued member of society.

With that comes another thought. Suddenly everything the volunteering EU parents who are self-sufficient or work part time do is worth nothing. Money and money alone counts to be in. I volunteered endlessly over the last 15 years and that was my way of contributing to a better society, to give children the chance to take part in activities and to help society to flourish. I still see myself as part of our community. My husband is the main earner and we do not get benefits. However, should we need to say that we are not 'benefit scroungers' to be accepted? Anybody falling on hard time living here should be helped regardless of place of birth.

I have now started to pay the very expensive CSI as I love my children and husband and moving away is in my thoughts but not an option anymore. My daughter is a teenager. How can I expect her to leave her friends, education and sporting career behind to start all over in a new country? A country she only knows from a short holiday every summer. I am deeply disappointed and hurt by the short-sighted decision voters made when they voted Brexit and I think I will never get over that betrayal. The implications of Brexit will be felt by my family for many years to come.

M.B., Austria

PART III

*"I have hardly had a good night's sleep
since 24th June."*

When I was little, I used to lie awake at night thinking where I would hide when the Gestapo came. It was ridiculous and historically inaccurate – the war had ended thirty years earlier. But my ears had been filled with stories of my parents' wartime childhood, of bullets whizzing past, of partisans hiding in a cupboard, of hunger and cold. I read Anne Frank's *Diary* before going to sleep and asked myself how long could I lie still if they came looking for me.

Recently, I had a dream that took me right back to those years. Except that this time it is not the Gestapo but men with tattooed arms and very short haircuts who break into my home, throw my clothes on the street and tell me never to come back. The dream is so obvious – and stereotypical – that I'm embarrassed by it. Yet it tells me that I am an EU citizen in the UK in the year 2016, and my subconscious thinks I'm Anne Frank in 1940s Amsterdam.

My family is multi-national, a three-passport concoction, a mini-EU. I'm Italian, of Greek-Italian parentage; my husband is Dutch, our daughter is gloriously, incongruously British; or as she puts it, 'half-Dutch, a quarter Italian, a quarter Greek – and a 100% English'. My husband and I met here, in England, in 1990, when I came as an Erasmus student. We married here, our daughter was born here. English is the lingua franca in our family: we fight in it, swear in it, love in it, dream in it. There is for us no other country where we all belong, in subtly different and yet roughly equivalent ways. I know because we tried.

Until June, we had plans; now everything is on hold. We bought a house earlier this year, which I don't dare to furnish in case we have to leave. I have stopped unpacking the boxes. My husband needs to start applying for a renewal of the grant that funds his programme of research right now. But should he? Or should he consider a position elsewhere? We don't know.

I look at my daughter sleeping and wonder if our family will be split up, how I'd cope with being a Skype mummy, how would we explain it to her. She is a citizen of the country that might want to expel her parents, of a country that refuses to guarantee her parents' right to stay. How devastating would that be for her sense of her place in the world? At best she would have to leave with us – losing her school, her friends, her world. We try to shield her as much as possible. But one day she comes home with a form asking for her nationality and language. It's for the school census; there is a campaign to boycott it. I agonise whether I should too, feeling vulnerable and exposed whichever way I choose.

On a good day, I believe the guarantees cannot but come, soon, and we will then be able to resume our suspended lives, to make plans, to become normal citizens again. It is impossible to return to a world where countries are only made up of one nationality (which the UK never was anyway) and national identities are simple and uncomplicated, unless by an act of violence. How would you separate the different components of our family, of my daughter's identity, of my lingering affection for this beautiful country, of my husband's contribution to its scientific reputation?

On a bad day, like today, like yesterday, I look at the pictures coming out of Aleppo, and realise how little human lives matter in high-stake politics. I lie awake at night again, holding my breath, listening to the sounds outside. Looking for signs, reading the runes.

In the meantime, we wait.

Elena Gualtieri, Italy

★★★

When I moved to Oxford to do a postdoc and later as a senior lecturer, my initial impression of the UK was one of openness and cosmopolitan – a stark contrast with Belgian academia, which I experienced as being more closed off.

As we've been renting, moving over ten times the past 15 years, we were eager to buy a house in Oxfordshire. We want a place to call home, and believed the UK could be that place. But now, since the Referendum in which we had no say, the plan of buying a house is off. We don't know if we can stay here, or if our rights will remain intact, for instance, to work here, to use the NHS, or even whether our children can continue to attend school. Because our family left the UK for 11 months over the past five years, we do not qualify for permanent residency. Not a day goes by that I do not think about this. The UK keeps on shifting the goal posts for permanent residency and citizenship. I worry that even if we are allowed to stay, the UK could reverse its decision several years down the line and I would still not have my rights secured with PR and citizenship forever out of reach.

While people here are friendly and supportive, I think they do not have a good sense of how emotionally draining this is. My line manager said that if getting permanent residency is so difficult, why not go for British citizenship? He had no idea that permanent residency is a prerequisite for citizenship, nor that citizenship requires tests and fees in excess of £1000. Some people even tell me I should not mention my situation. For instance, one woman blamed me for spoiling the mood, and bringing politics into a discussion where I made a joke about being deported. She said she voted out but of course I was allowed to stay, as far as she's concerned. My biggest worry is that we are the UK's main negotiation card (by the government's own admission), and so that if negotiations go badly we could end up becoming collateral damage.

Last year my father-in-law died. He was a hobby painter, and he left us a painting of one of his favourite places, a little cabin in the Swiss Alps. Now, we cannot hang the painting as it is heavy and would leave a mark in the wall. We were going to hang it in our first home. But now it remains wrapped in bubble-wrap and blankets, a symbol of our lives on hold, and a reminder that we cannot call the UK home. Where is home? I used to believe that home is where the heart is, not necessarily where you are born. Now, my heart is no longer in the UK, and so as a result I feel emotionally homeless.

Dr Helen De Cruz, Belgium

★★★

In 1966 I married someone in the British army who was stationed in Germany. He was posted back to Britain, where I have lived since 1967. Before moving to London I had been working as a multi-lingual secretary in Amsterdam and also for a while in Germany. On arrival in London it was easy to find a good job in the European Office of an American company. Although I enjoyed working in an international set-up with colleagues from USA, France, the Netherlands and UK, it was a culture shock coming to UK. In the late sixties, London still had many bomb sites, it was dirty, damp and grey. I was homesick for my family, my friends and Amsterdam.

After three years I had a lovely, healthy little boy, but my marriage was difficult and it did not last. In 1974 I took my courage in both hands and became a single parent – I could not return to the Netherlands with my son because of custody arrangements and I had to make the best of life in Britain for my son and myself, without any family nearby. However, with the help of a few good friends, some offering shelter and others practical assistance and the long distance support from my parents, sister and Dutch friends, I was eventually able to find some-where safe to live and a job in a local NHS hospital with a crèche for pre-school children. It broke my heart to leave my precious son there while I was at work. However, before long the children of my (mostly foreign like me) colleagues, nurses, doctors and therapists at my place of work, became my son's friends and I in turn became friends with many of the parents. Just before I left the NHS after about seven years and totally unexpectedly, I met someone who wanted to spend the rest of his life with me and the feeling was mutual. We got together in 1981 and never looked back.

Life was not always easy, but the three of us were together, loving and secure. Both my husband and I worked hard, he in the NHS and I in public housing. I had become totally immersed in British culture and its way of life.

While working I studied part time (all self-financed) initially with the Open University, then a part-time MA at the University of Kent and later in 2000 a part-time BA Hon in Visual Arts at Chelsea College of Art. Although my heritage is Dutch, I love living in Britain. I identify more with the UK than the Netherlands. However, I still have a Dutch passport. It never occurred to me that at the age of 75 and having lived here for fifty years, being Dutch could one day make me 'the other'. Not because I felt different, but because others might start to see me differently.

The Leave vote came as a tremendous shock to me – I woke up at 4 am on the 24th of July and thought to just quickly see the result of the Referendum and then go back to sleep. I can honestly say that I have hardly had a good night's sleep since. I wake up after two or three hours' sleep, actively worrying about where to find proof of my 50 years of life and work in Britain and even if I were to get PR, for how long would that keep me safe? Because I am a widow, my Dutch passport would be taken away from me if I obtained British nationality. According to the Dutch authorities, my 30 year marriage has supposedly been 'dissolved' because of my husband's death five years ago.

The fact that he is buried nearby, that my (British) only son lives nearby, all my friends and support systems and the people I give support to are here in UK, seems to suddenly count for nothing. This is only a potted history and may sound negative. However, although I do not know what the future holds, I shall fight to the end to help and bring this divisive and ill-thought out Brexit madness to an end.

Elly Wright, The Netherlands

★★★

The NHS does not always have the best reputation, but the NHS has featured and features large in my life. Since the Referendum I'm wondering if it will be possible to get treatment or care should become ill, disabled or old in this country. I hope that I will age joyfully.

I came from Germany to the UK to train as an occupational therapist. I have had many opportunities to develop my career here, including studying for a Master's degree in rehabilitation, an opportunity I would not have had in Germany at the time. I have since worked for many years as an occupational therapist, enabling patients to live their daily lives and to return to their homes. Mid-career I decided to work in higher education as a lecturer teaching healthcare students, and to work as a researcher. I loved my work, but it was demanding and challenging at times.

I was working in a stroke unit, when I met my husband who was doing a locum at the hospital. This year I will be married for 30 years. We have three children who grew up here. I call the UK my home, but I also feel very connected to the part of Germany where I grew up.

A few years ago I was diagnosed with cancer. I had many months of active treatment. It is an interesting experience being on the 'other side'. Whilst being treated I could not travel abroad. I found that thought very difficult. What if I do not make it and never see my German family? I know it is an irrational thought, but I wondered if my soul can rest in this country. In so many ways I was lucky that the staff at the hospital were very kind and I felt in very safe hands.

Since the Referendum I have been feeling quite destabilised. It has unleashed an existential angst in me. A cancer diagnosis brings a lot of uncertainty about the future. The Referendum brought another layer of uncertainty, especially not knowing if in the future I will still have access to the NHS. I have over 30 years of National Insurance contributions, but will they count? I know how important specialist healthcare can be, and what a difference it can make. I also know that specialist care and especially cancer care is very expensive. Losing access to the NHS could mean not being able to afford treatment and bankrupting my family. I have considered moving back to Germany, but my husband and children are here, so moving is not an easy option.

Doro Bechinger-English, Germany

★★★

I have dual nationality. My father was a Spaniard that fled the Spanish civil war. So I hold both Argentinian and Spanish passports. I came here less than five years ago: two years and a half to be precise. When I knew that there was going to be a Referendum I panicked.

I couldn't apply for PR but I did apply for a registration certificate before the Referendum. Some people say it's useless. I consider it to be a document issued by the government stating that I am here in good terms, contributing, exercising treaty rights, before the Referendum. There are talks about recognising who's been here before or after a cut-off date.

It doesn't feel great when the government stated that the case of those living less than five years will be at the centre of negotiations.

My main concern is to be treated the same as how the government currently treats non-EU nationals. Non-EU nationals have specific visas and cannot switch categories otherwise their time in the UK resets and they have to start all over again with another category. And that an EU document of residence costs £65 whereas visas for non-EU citizens are over £1000, limited in time and as complicated as getting PR!

When I came here I did so as a student. Back then I decided to take a yearly travel insurance policy in the case of an emergency. Just in case. In hindsight, I didn't fully understand that having comprehensive sickness insurance was a requirement to be legally studying in the UK as an EU national. Even so, I run the risk of being told that it is not sufficient enough if in a future I want to apply for PR.

After finishing my postgraduate studies, I found myself being a job seeker. During that time, I have never used public funds or claimed benefits. I just lived of my own savings. I put all my efforts to get my current job. Despite having a master's degree in finance I was told, "I don't understand your qualifications... You don't have experience in the UK, so you have to be flexible in salary and location."

It hurts to see nowadays rhetoric. People claiming to 'put British workers first', 'train our own people', 'kick unskilled immigrants out' or talking about 'birth rights taken away'. I have spent so far more than ten years of my life studying and working to be an actuary. Sometimes I imagine myself giving them my bulky study notes and saying, "alright then, here you go, train yourself."

To give a background, an actuary applies mathematical models and techniques to manage risk, establish reserves and project future cash flows for banks, insurance companies and other financial institutions. Back to reality, because I had to pay the bills, I got into an unskilled job as a bartender. That didn't last long. After having some interviews I got a job as an actuarial analyst. I do really like my job.

All this couldn't have happened without my Spanish nationality, freedom of movement and its flexibility. That flexibility of switching categories of residency could be lost after Brexit. I would feel very sad because all this will probably be curtailed as a result of the UK leaving the EU. Since the Referendum result sometimes I work loads more than before. I feel that I have to justify not being made redundant if a visa was required. I also feel much more anxious and worried about what the future holds.

All I'm told is, "wait and see." But living in limbo is not a good place to be and I don't wish that to anyone. I wholeheartedly hope a fair deal for everyone involved comes soon.

Manuel Ignacio Fernandez Orellana, Spain/Argentina

★★★

I'm lucky to live in Brighton which is a very tolerant and open-minded city. Being German is sometimes an obstacle – being gay is yet another one. Ever since the 23rd June 2016 I am feeling uneasy about the place I have called home for the last twenty years and it is only down to my British partner (we are married) that I have not left the UK to go back to Germany.

What really annoys me is the fact that some of the British media keeps focussing on the worst of Germany by showing films about its dark past again and again. On at least two occasions every week, there are reports about the Nazis and all the terrible things that happened over seventy years ago. Unfortunately, however, the world hasn't learnt any lessons from the past and history will, and actually is, repeating itself – even in this country because there are people who are riding on the back of Brexit and assume it is now correct to be racist/homophobic/xenophobic and so on. Unless we condemn them, this negative development will continue and we should do everything we can to make sure we are living in a tolerant society and don't turn into brainless sheep being influenced constantly by the media.

Wolfie, Germany

★★★

In 1990 I married a wonderful British man and we decided to live in the UK. We were blessed with two children and I chose to stay at home to look after our family whilst my husband worked in the NHS.

Because of the freedom of movement within the EU I never had to go through any red tape in order to live here as a foreign national. I was given a NHS number and a NI number without any problem and could live like any British citizen. I never encountered xenophobia, on the contrary, I have always felt welcome here and acquired many wonderful British friends.

The day after the Referendum was a shock; I never thought we would actually leave the EU but it was staring me in the face and it felt like a physical blow. I managed to put it in the back of my mind after a while, thinking that it wouldn't directly have an impact on me personally, after all I was married to a Brit. How wrong can you be! At the beginning of this year I read a few newspaper articles that woke me up and I started to realise all was not well.

In order to get the piece of paper proving the right of PR, you need to go through a lengthy application, which I was willing to do. However, I discovered that I would not qualify due to a requirement that I had never ever heard of: it's called Comprehensive Sickness Insurance.

As I rely on my husband's income I am classed as self-sufficient. Since 2004 those self-sufficient people have to have a CSI in order to live here lawfully. Except nobody ever bothered to tell us! All of a sudden we realised I am in fact living in the UK unlawfully and cannot apply for PR or British Citizenship! We cannot afford a CSI but even if we could, I think it is an unfair and discriminatory requirement, which should be scrapped.

You might think, 'Why don't you get a job, surely, you would be okay then?' Even if I would be able to get a job right now, I still would not be able to apply for PR for five years and by that time the UK will have left the EU!

So however you turn this thing (and trust me I have!) I am left in no-man's land, unable to legitimise my existence in this country. There are many questions that are unanswered and despite my efforts not to worry it is there every day. It feels as if my life is hijacked by the government!

I might not be able to stay despite having lived here for 26 years, having a British husband and two British children. Maybe they won't deport me but will they make our life just too difficult so we simply cannot stay? Can I come back home into the country after a trip abroad? Will I be able to access healthcare? Will I be able to get a job?

I have no life to go back to in the Netherlands, I've made my life here and would like to continue to do so. It would break my heart if I had to leave. I can't wait till the day we are all legally assured of our rights to reside in this country without exceptions or discriminatory rules.

Marlies Haselton, The Netherlands

★★★

I've probably been here shorter than most people, but I moved to Oxford in 2015 to study. I worked and studied since I moved to Oxford to support myself (I never once even claimed a grant, bursary or loan from the

UK government). I made friends from all over the world and graduated from my MSc with a distinction. I even got accepted to do a PhD at the same university and decided to stay.

We are nearing the one year mark since the Referendum and though I don't want to leave (as I love my friends, studies and job here), I worry about what is to come. I would love to stay and successfully complete my PhD, but I have been stressing about stories of students that are being asked to leave because of legal loopholes. I have applied for a registration certificate this week and I hope I will receive it within the next few months. The uncertainty takes energy and attention that would be better spent on my studies.

Sebastiaan Marcus Elizabeth Raymaekers, Belgium

★★★

So finally after months of waiting and the last few weeks full of discussions, heated arguments and tears we have come to a decision. My British husband is still hopeful that things will be fine after Brexit and doesn't want to leave his job here in the UK yet. So instead of putting all our eggs into one basket we have decided to have one foot into each country for a while.

We will sell our UK house first. Hubby will stay here and find some lodgings. The children and I will move to France (my home country) and settle there in rented accommodation. I don't know how long for we will be apart, but I don't want to stay here anymore and hubby doesn't want to leave his job at the moment. He has worked hard to get where he is in his job and he doesn't want to move to France to "go back 20 years and lose what he has built here," he said. His French is poor, his job is not a transferable job, he doesn't feel confident that he can learn the language well enough to get a decent employment abroad and in any case he feels that Brexit might not turn out to be a disaster.

Sadly I cannot share his optimism with my precarious status being a constant black cloud... Unfortunately, I am not one of the skilled immigrants this government wants. I am currently an unwell stay-at-home mum without PR and I don't want to wait like a sitting duck for another two years. Nine months of uncertainty and worries since last June is all I can take.

There was never going to be an easy solution due to our personal circumstances. Moving to France won't be a simple task and I am anxious because I have lost touch with France since I have been in the UK for 26 years now and I have never lived in France as an adult.

I'm very sad and upset that we will be a Skype family for some time and the children will certainly miss their dad, I anticipate tears and fears on their part. But by leaving rather sooner than later I can settle the children in France before our eldest begins secondary school and I hope to get better medical treatment in my home country. I have a chronic condition and due to its crumbling state the NHS has been way too slow with appointments, diagnosis decisions and treatment options and this has kept me unable to work for the past year. I am fairly confident with the right treatment I could get well enough to get back to work. Because my health isn't good I worry a lot about my right to access the NHS post-Brexit. This also is a significant reason about my decision to leave the UK since I cannot find a CSI insurer that will cover my pre-existing conditions.

When I look at my present life in the UK now apart from my husband, my children and our mortgaged house I have nothing left in this country. When I got ill half of my so-called friends deserted me. Brexit is making me stressed and is impacting further on my health. My husband's family are Brexiters, I'm deeply unhappy about seeing them anymore. And I have fallen out of love with the UK. This is us now trying to make the best out of a bad situation.

Nathalie, France

★★★

After obtaining my first degree in Italy, I studied for a Masters in Philosophy at King's College London. I was not funded at all to start with and grateful for my parents who paid my student fees. For extra money, I did some waitressing in cafés at lunchtime and at functions in the evening. I also worked as a shop assistant at Clinton cards. I got my Masters with distinction and moved to do a BPhil in Oxford. By this time, I got a small scholarship from Bologna University as a contribution for studying abroad and a college scholarship covering my college fees. My family helped with university fees, and I continued to work, from market research to night shifts in the library, babysitting, etc. I also volunteered for Oxfam and fully participated in the life of the college, contributed to student societies, etc. I passed and wanted to do a PhD but could no longer cope without funding, so I moved to Australia where I got a full scholarship for three years.

I moved back to the UK in 2004 after getting my PhD and applied for jobs. I taught for a year in a sixth-form college and then started my academic career: first a research associate position in Manchester and then a permanent lectureship in Birmingham. Now I am a Professor of Philosophy at the University of Birmingham, I live in London with my partner and we have two daughters. My oldest was born in Italy but did all her schooling in the UK and my youngest was born in London. We see London as home and have most of our social lives there, although we go back to Italy often to see family and we travel for work a bit. I have had some modest success with research funding before, but in 2013 I had a break-through: I was awarded an ERC Consolidator Grant (prestigious and generous funding from the European Research Council). Because of it, I was able to form a team and my university hired five full-time members of staff (two funded PhD students and three post-docs) with the European funding I had obtained. Four out of five are UK nationals.

Even for someone like me, privileged in many ways for having had a permanent job for 12 years, applying for residence is not a walk in the park due to two periods of maternity leave and frequent travel abroad. The form is difficult to understand and imposes unreasonable demands. We will probably go through the process as a family, but it is a major undertaking and source of stress and worry. I gave birth to my second daughter in June 2016 and spent the first few weeks of her life preparing for the Life in the UK test, late at night, while nursing. This is how much the Referendum and its outcome affected our lives. And I am sure the worst is still to come.

Professor Lisa Bortolotti, Italy

★★★

When my country joined the EEA in 1994 I came here to study and work. I finished my first postgraduate, and was all set to happily go home when practically in the last five minutes I met my British husband. So I stayed.

Family circumstances meant that we could never really consider moving to my country. I built a life here, had two beautiful daughters, studied for a PhD and embarked on a successful career. Won't consider dual citizenship because my country won't allow it, and I don't want to burn all bridges. Have applied for PR but unfortunately, Royal Mail have lost my application, so no idea how this story is going to end. I no longer sleep because of worry.

I am also so extremely upset because of the nature of information that needs to be submitted. So much private detail – how much money I have earned, what's in my bank account, what is my house worth, what did the NHS write to me about... To think that, since it is presumed missing, all this is accessible to strangers and potentially in unauthorised hands makes me feel quite ill.

Kristina Standeven, Austria

★★★

I moved to UK last July. I have always wanted to move to London, but only 18 months ago I was able to make the biggest decision of my life. It took me a year to organise everything, from a secure, very low-paid job and two teenage daughters in Italy, to the new life I had always wanted. I had started an online course to become a Specialist Dyslexia Teacher. I had given up my job, called the movers.

Imagine my shock on the morning of 24th June! Our things almost all packed up, the movers coming in a week's time. I couldn't stay in Italy because I had no job in September, so I decided to move anyway. After all, I had spent a lot of money on the Dyslexia Teacher course. I later found out that only the UK has this professional profile, so I can only work in the UK.

My partner was supposed to come at a later stage because his situation is so difficult that he cannot afford to move here now. Due to the uncertainties of the Brexit he never will. So it is just my daughters and I.

My girls have told me that they don't want to go back to Italy. On the other hand, I have a partner in Italy who cannot come now amid the present Brexit uncertainties. So I am torn between my partner and my girls.

This is what the Brexit meant for me. To work in the position I am training for and to give my daughters a future, I have to give up my partner, the love of my life, because you cannot keep a relationship going if you are together three times a year for just a few days.

I wake up every morning and I go to bed every night crying because this is an impossible choice. Thank you for taking the time to read my story.

A.L., Italy

★★★

I have three children, all British, the youngest has just turned 20. I have lived in the UK for over 30 years and worked all of my life, taking time off to bring up my children, or going part-time as required.

I am now disabled, and every day I read more stories about people's rights not being guaranteed once we leave the EU, the more I fear for my future in the UK. I never thought that I would be seen as a burden to this country. I never thought that I would have to worry about being a carer for my autistic son. I never believed that being born in another country would ever make any difference to what would become of me and my family in my later years.

I feel trapped: I do not have the means to leave this country now or later, but I fear I will be told I have to go, and leave my son behind, then my husband would have to stop working to look after our son, and we wouldn't be a family anymore. What would become of me? I don't belong in my native country any more, this here is my home.

I keep on thinking this is a bad dream and that my adoptive country wouldn't reject me, wouldn't see me as a useless burden, would never lose its collective humanity to the point they would treat foreign disabled people as something to get rid of, counting our value only in monetary terms.

I don't say it to my friends, because I don't think they realise how worried I am, and they won't take my fears seriously; it all sounds so melodramatic when you say it aloud, doesn't it? But it eats at me all the time, even as I try to just get on with it.

This is what Brexit has done to me: it's taken the solid ground I was standing on and has turned my future into uncertainty. As we were heading quietly towards retirement, it has created a wall of uncertainty, and it is making me feel mentally ill. That's the reality of Brexit for me.

Anonymous, France

Have you heard the one about the British woman who married an immigrant just so she could leave the country? That's the 'joke' that I've been telling, ever since June 24th last year, when I woke up in some kind of parallel universe to find that my compatriots had voted to leave the EU. But I'm not laughing – and neither are the thousands of other people in the UK who are in a similar situation.

My partner, Mickaël, father of our 19-month-old daughter, Sidonie, is French – an EU immigrant. As things now stand, he might not be allowed to stay in the UK. Going to live in France – assuming the British will still have rights and I'll be welcome there - might be the only way we can stay together as a family. Exile from my homeland or the break-up of my family: it's not a pleasant choice.

When Mickaël and I met, having a relationship with an EU citizen was (aside from the air miles and the language difference) little different from dating the boy next door. I had gone out to Nice to write a book; he worked at the apart-hotel I was staying in. For the first few years, we conducted our relationship as a long-distance one, taking advantage of low-cost flights to hop backwards and forwards across the Channel before, in 2014, deciding to settle down together and start a family.

Mickaël moved to London primarily because I have a mortgage and because his English is better than my French. Immigrating for him, as for other EU arrivals, was as simple as getting on a plane, opening a bank account, registering with the local GP and securing a National Insurance number. And yet, two years after he gave up his home and his job and learned to play the theme tune to The Archers on his harmonica, he was told 'Sorry, but you're no longer welcome here and you might not be able to stay.'

To date, Prime Minister Theresa May has refused to guarantee the rights of EU citizens in the UK until those of UK citizens living in Europe are also guaranteed. But this game of chicken and egg is messing not only with the lives and futures of Europeans, but also with the very British lives she claims to wish to protect. What she has failed to acknowledge is that EU immigrants do not live in ghettos in the UK. The three million are intimately connected with British people, as their partners, their parents, their siblings, their grandparents. They have mortgages together, businesses together, children together. My rights and those of my daughter, also a British citizen, are being threatened by May's refusal to promise EU immigrants that they can stay. According to Article 8 of the Human Rights Act – which the government hasn't yet done away with – we are entitled a family life. So why isn't she ensuring this? My family is particularly vulnerable. Mickaël has lived here for less than three years and is therefore not yet entitled to PR or citizenship (you qualify after five years). He is not highly skilled. In fact, he is exactly the kind of immigrant we're told the country neither needs nor wants. Except I want and need him. And his daughter wants and needs her Papa too.

I haven't slept very well since June 24th. I'm still shocked and anxious and depressed by what has happened, grieving for the country I thought I lived in, for my identity and for the future I was promised. I'm scared for my family's future. Most of all I'm angry. You could say I have a giant bargaining-shaped chip on my shoulder. I feel like I've been lied to all of my life, taught to think of myself as European, to take advantage of free movement, only to have the door slammed in my face at the age of 45. Even my educational choices were made because of the EU, my school persuading me to choose French A level 'because the 1992 Maastricht Treaty means the whole of Europe will be opening up for your generation'.

You might think I'm overreacting (or as the right wing press would have it, that I'm a Remoaner). Most people do. 'Don't worry,' they say. 'Everything will be fine.' I see no evidence of this. Eight months on, and the three million EU immigrants are still being used as pawns in a political game with no discernible rules, whose players make their moves according to 'the will of the people.' EU families have had no assurances, we have been shown no compassion. The second thing people say to me is: 'If you're worried about Mickaël not being able to stay, why don't you just get married?' Contrary to popular opinion, being married will grant Mickaël no automatic right to live in the UK. The law quietly changed back in 2015, you see, when the then Home Secretary – a certain Theresa May – decided to put a stop to immigrants marrying Brits just so they could stay here.

Don't underestimate the levels of misery and fear Brexit has generated. Some people were actually scared to talk to me when I wrote a piece for The Guardian newspaper for fear that being quoted in this article would mean their names would find their way on to a government list, and they'd be deported. This level of paranoia, whether it is warranted or not, in 21st Century Britain, is deeply shocking.

Whatever happens to Mickaël and me, at least our daughter Sidonie, who is now beginning to speak both English and French, will be able to live freely in whichever country she chooses. She is a dual national, entitled to both passports. As the granddaughter of German Jewish Holocaust refugees, I am currently in the process of obtaining a German passport, so that if I do have to move to France, I will still be an EU citizen with whatever rights that grants me. Even if Mickaël were to be offered PR in the UK, that status would be revoked if he left the country for longer than a few months. The consequence of this is that we would not be able take our daughter to live in France to experience French culture and to embrace the French half of her identity. That is why, for us, as for many other thousands of people who don't wish to see the break-up of their mixed UK/EU families, only Free Movement will do. Otherwise, one partner will find themselves, whether willingly or unwillingly, forever exiled in the other's nation.

Hilary Freeman, UK

★★★

I came from Italy for a week holiday in November 1997 and ended up staying here.

I started to work part time as sales assistant just to get a bit better at the language while studying at university, and when I finished my CIPD, I worked in Human Resources roles and also as self-employed.

In 1999 I got married to another EU citizen, and continued to work until 2002 when my first child was born, and then I decided to stay home to take care of my daughter. Following my husband's work we lived from 2004 to 2010 in Italy and moved back for good in UK in August 2010. We bought a house and settled well in Greater London, our children were born here and they go to local state schools, they have friends and their life and their culture is English. In 2014 we adopted a little boy, he is British by birth and has British passport.

Myself and my husband have tried to apply twice for the permanent permit but it has been refused to both of us, because my husband has gap in his employment history and in his self-employed period has not private insurance. Also mine has been rejected as I do not have continuous five years of employment and no private insurance.

Like many other EU citizens we are in disbelief of this reckless attitude of the UK government toward us and the difficulties and obstacles to obtain a permanent residence card seem created by a very unfriendly anti-European feeling.

We are seriously worried of our possible future in UK and above all of that of our kids here, our son is the only British citizen in our family what will be the scenario after Brexit is ratified and the deals with the other country are settled? What about our own house, our life here and my husband's job? We will be obliged to leave everything behind and leave in a hurry?

Of course we have experienced acts of pure xenophobia and racist toward us and our EU friends, the phrase 'go back home' has been said to us several times. 'Britain belongs to British not you'. And since Brexit we have noticed a surge of very aggressive comments about not being civilised as British people are or not to be at the same level as British are.

It is heart-breaking and emotionally upsetting this incertitude about our future, the future of our kids and the atmosphere we are living in. Being treated as a bargain chip, ignored and undervalued and object of racism make me and my family frightened and shaken. But unfortunately we cannot do anything to secure our stay here and the only thing left is to wish and pray for a mighty Brexit deal about EU citizen in UK.

B.A., Italy

★★★

I fell in love with Brighton, and then with an English boy (who's now pushing 50!), having come for a week's stay as a language student. I was 18. I started work in hotels, then studied part time and am now a professional with a Master's degree. I work in the public sector to help deliver essential services for the most vulnerable – not easy with the cuts we are facing. I am sociable, outgoing and confident.

Since the Referendum, I have slowly but surely become withdrawn from my British friends and colleagues – not a problem with acquaintances who are happy with the result, but sad and difficult with those close to me. They do have good intentions, feel ashamed and embarrassed – but I find it so draining to have to respond to comments such as: 'you'll be fine, this isn't about you', ' but you've been here for ages', 'but you're a public servant' and my personal favourite so far: 'but you're normal, surely this doesn't apply to you'. So it's been easier to avoid the subject.

And then, the amendments to Article 50 were rejected by the House of Lords – I was left in tears. The morning after, I had planned to work from home to avoid people as I felt really resentful and angry at everything and everyone, as well as tearful. Not a healthy and or sustainable way to deal with what is going on. So I decided that instead of dwelling on things and staying in that state of mind I would look ahead: I'm losing friends? So what – I have made lots of new ones since connecting with fellow EU citizens. I might upset friends and colleagues if I'm too honest – so what? I feel bruised and I'm dealing with it, they can deal with and act upon their own feelings – I matter just as much as they do.

I want to be back in control – my world has completely changed over the last few months, I have no idea what my future holds anymore. I'm not going to stop fighting and I want to be heard – I am one of many and I matter. I refuse to feel like a powerless victim – I don't like it. So I went into work with my new attitude on and to my amazement had a very positive discussion with my colleagues. So yes, my world has changed but I can and will influence my future.

Carole Convers, France

★★★

Last November, I had a few moments before and during the Society for Neuroscience meeting and I thought I'd write down a few reflections about the politically catastrophic 2016. I have always made it clear that Brexit and then Trump are what I consider abject failures of reason and the results of the post-fact era. This topic is so vast that I'm at serious risk of digressing a lot so I will concentrate on why is it that I feel these two events are so personal to me.

For me, they herald not only the end of era of reason but a likely beginning of a disassembly of a post-cold war frame of reference and the security it offered. I remember APVs and battle tanks during the winter of '82 on the street junction where my daycare was. My parents' chats about whether ageing and paranoid Andropov would unleash war on us. Able Archer and Reagan's rhetoric didn't help much either. Since I was 4 years old, I thought for a number of years that war was something imminent. It was largely due to WW2 being as real as it gets for my grandparents and parents, and shaping their world view. It was almost a daily topic for me. Luckily, Andropov died quickly enough, Chernenko was somewhat less belligerent, detente followed and eventually 1989 arrived. Systems changed, hope arrived. For me and many I know the broadly-defined West really was the shining city on the hill. The likes of NATO and the EU offered the prospect of finally being safe and prosperous and this was the raison d'être back then – nation-wide and personal. Lo and behold, it somehow panned out. Poland's accession to NATO and later the EU were momentous for me.

Around that time I went to Germany, I got an EU-funded stipend, finished a PhD, working at the Max-Planck Institute in Goettingen with some of the most brilliant people I have ever met. They were from everywhere in the world and this was the best formative experience I could have asked for. My course fellows and friends were mostly migrants – from Poland, Lesotho, Trinidad, Ireland, Russia, Ukraine, Taiwan, Spain, Italy, Israel, Romania and Switzerland. When I finished my studies, I wrapped up the German chapter of my life and went to Northern Ireland to work for a cutting-edge high-tech company – one of maybe five or six globally – and it has become my home ever since. I love the Northern Irish, their self-deprecating sense of humour, their positive outlook on life – even with all the multi-faceted and often heart-breaking baggage of The Troubles. I have always felt welcome and accepted here – a place where I could spend my entire life.

Fast forward eleven years and then comes Brexit (Northern Ireland voted to Remain) fuelled by many resentments and as many blatant lies. Some of these lies were so simplistic that I still struggle to understand how they got so popular (£350m/week for the NHS, immigrants' drain on the budget etc.).

It was an ideological vote and seemingly no volume of data could address ideas of "the immigrants coming over here, taking jobs and getting benefits".

What makes me most concerned is the fact that few people with whom I spoke about this saw the EU institutions primarily as peacekeeping mechanisms. Only one friend hailing from Bulgaria also saw the potential collapse of the EU as a clear and present danger to European and wider global peace. For me this is the most crucial issue. It has only been twenty-seven years of my belonging to the shining city on the hill, and the thought of it being deconstructed by the likes of Farage, Gove, Putin, Le Pen, AfD, PiS, Fidesz and their ilk fills me with dread.

So this is why I find the current situation so depressing. Although the collective memory of what wars did to us in Europe has now proved to be very short, it all happened not that long ago.

Dr Marcin Barszczewski, Poland

★★★

Being foreign in London was never a problem in the twenty years I have lived here – this city is one of the most tolerant I have come across in my life. I think that Londoners in general are perfectly fine being surrounded by people of different backgrounds and nationalities.

However, something odd happened to me a couple of weeks ago while I was on the Piccadilly line. I was chatting with a friend of mine in Italian. Suddenly, this lady that was sitting opposite us looked like she wanted to talk to us. We stopped to listen to her and it turned out she was upset with us. She said we were making noise (we were not screaming or talking loud) and that she was bothered by us speaking in a foreign language. My friend could not believe what she was hearing and asked me in Italian to confirm that the lady was disturbed by us talking in Italian. The lady went on and on saying that we were rude and should speak in English. She became increasingly agitated, going on and on, getting more and more angry with us. We carried on talking in Italian, telling each other that in all these years in London nothing on this scale had ever happened to us. I think it's not good for London and it doesn't do justice to a city that is one of the most open in the world. But sadly it is also happening here.

One English friend told me that in my area you can hear many different accents and that there are too many foreigners there – he seemed a little bit annoyed about that. I fear more racist and abusive comments could be just around the corner. This is just the top of the iceberg underneath.

L.S., Italy

★★★

I've got a British boyfriend, an international household, a community of friends, an artistic career. I left Poland because it was conservative, sexist, racist, intolerant. I escaped small-town mentality and conservative nosiness into London in 2012, only to find that Britain has those things, too. While there are major differences (Polish anti-discrimination laws are 'barely there' and rarely enforced besides, and the mentality is very different), looks like prejudice is a universal human quality. It feels like the bullies followed me home – or home away from home.

I came to London to be creative; to unlearn prejudice by living in a diverse society; to find my tribe, places and people where I can belong. And I did and found all those things. And then in June a young guy harassing me on the Tube called me "a f*cking European". It was two weeks before the Referendum and I wanted him to leave me alone; he was drunk enough not to take the hint. When I finally swore, he said, "Brexit! The sooner the better!" as if my rejection was a perfect opportunity to decide all foreigners are bad. It was the first time I realised that something had changed.

I started reading up on politics. I incorporated that incident into my stand-up comedy, trying to make people laugh and think. I co-hosted the 'Jobstealers' Podcast' – desperately trying to find a voice, have a voice. I went to see 'My Country' at the National Theatre – migrant perspective is so irrelevant to the concept of Britain that it was all but absent. I didn't know what to do, so I talked, wrote and talked some more – I wrote a review of the play (to no reaction) and I'm working on my own theatre work, too. Any way I can say something, because nobody's asking us – and we're human, these are our lives. We will bear the consequences of these actions and we have to take every opportunity to speak up.

I don't have the answers. It feels so wrong that a referendum took place at all, that a disenchanted public could vote my rights away, such a complex situation dealt with via a yes or no question. Sometimes I still can't believe that it happened. It does beg the question – how to make Europe? How would we like the EU to work to offer fair unencumbered opportunities? Should we become a European nation, so that one nation can't decide the fate of others?

But these are lofty questions when your personal life is affected. Often I don't know what to do. I can't afford citizenship. I've been here since graduating at university, I never even paid taxes in Poland. Here is where my jobs were and are, where my community is, my life. I'm dusting off my German, highly aware that my relationship might not survive if I'm forced to leave – I'd be asking a lot of my partner, a native Brit whose entire life and career is here. I have no children, I'm relatively free of obligations and so have it easier than most... but I worry about the future. Britain's choices affect us all and Brexit has already messed with my mental health. It feels like living under a threat, all the time. A sword of Damocles, which will eventually fall.

Rita Suszek, Poland

★★★

My son married an English girl. They courted for three years and we kept in touch with their parents as well. After marriage however the parents sent a verbal message that they don't want to see us anymore. Me and my husband are from Hungary but have been living here for 30 years. My daughter in law with her nose up also behaved strangely: polite middle class tolerance.

It has actually happened after Brexit and of course they voted Brexit. My son is afraid of losing his wife's support, does not dare to stand up for his family so we don't keep in touch... I lost him. The other son is also courting an English girl. Actually when they moved my husband helped them to set up a wardrobe. He asked for a screwdriver in Hungarian language. The girl's father exclaimed: "Speak English. We are in England."

E., Hungary

★★★

I have been living in Scotland on and off since 1991, and permanently since 2002. Originally from Finland and married to a Scot for 22 years now. In the beginning I didn't want British citizenship as I would have lost my Finnish one. By the time the law changed I no longer felt any need for it, and didn't see any point spending money on it. How I now wish I had done it then!

Until the day of the vote last summer, I felt safe, happy and blissfully unaware that things could change so horribly and suddenly. I actually burst out crying when I found out the results in the morning. At the time my husband couldn't understand, he could not picture the whole horror straight away, but he has since gotten the idea.

For around nine months I tried to decide what to do, if anything, until I finally decided I wanted to apply for citizenship, as my life is here and I no longer feel safe. That's when I discovered I don't qualify. Actually I'm lucky compared to so many, as I will be able to apply in a few months, but it was a shock to realise that my years as a student and carer count for nothing.

The actual words by the Home Office upset me most, that as a carer I was a 'burden on society'. I looked after my (British) mother-in-law for more than 11 years after her stroke, in my home, on a 24/7 basis, she could do nothing for herself. While doing this I put myself through four years of university, which was only made possible by us personally paying for a carer for mum during my study time. Of course I had never heard of CSI.

It really annoys me when people say, "It's ok, they won't throw you out." No, probably not, but what about my health care, my pension, etc, will they be safe? Since I made my decision, and have been looking into it, I have started biting my nails, grinding my teeth, I had a migraine, and generally I have been very anxious and jumpy. Also very emotional. Again I'm lucky that I have the full support of my husband and family and friends, I have seen how much worse it can be for others who don't even have this. I refuse to give up. I will keep going till I have that invitation to my citizenship ceremony.

M. N., Finland

★★★

Every day I wake up and hope the Referendum result was just a bad dream. But it's not. I don't know if I will be allowed to stay or whether I will have the same rights after Brexit. I have not applied for PR as I do not have enough evidence of my qualifying years as a worker and I did not have CSI when I looked after my children as a self-sufficient person.

This uncertainty is driving me crazy, but I have to put my smile on every day and go to work amongst mainly British people who may or may not be Leavers, may or may not dislike immigrants. I've become suspicious and scared of going out with the children in case people hear me and become abusive. I've seen my child in tears when he got told to "F#<k off back to..."

I've never felt like an immigrant before. I was just 12 years old when I fell in love with the English language, British literature and culture. I was 21 when I met and fell in love with my wonderful British husband. I've spent so long in the UK that, when I tried to settle back in my country of birth with my husband and two children, I missed the UK so much, that I told my husband I wanted to go back home. And so we did. We came back to the UK exactly a year before the Referendum. Only now even the UK does not feel like home anymore.

Patrizia, Italy

★★★

I arrived in the UK September 2004. I wasn't the only one from my country and we had help with arranging NI number and bank account.

I worked for six years and was happy. It wasn't easy but it was good. I decided to quit my job and go to college for a year. Best decision ever! After that I was unemployed for four months and then I got a job in a call centre. Horrible job and the amount of abuse was enormous but it wasn't just me, we all had that. The colleagues were super! After five months I left to do a job I wanted to do since I moved to the UK and I am still doing this job.

All was well till the Referendum. I've not felt the same since. I don't feel safe anymore, I am nonstop on edge, afraid somebody will say anything about my accent.

I started applying for the PR card nearly straight away but I took my time so I would be sure I had all evidence I needed. I did get the card but instead of getting it over the first five years they've used the last five years. Probably because I didn't have CSI the year I went to college. Shouldn't have made a difference but clearly it has. It does worry me a bit as the date I required PR status is after the Referendum. We'll see if it is enough or not.

In January I had to call in sick. My anxiety was so bad I wasn't able to go into my own garden. Tomorrow, after three and a half months, I am going back to work. My boss has been really supportive and never pushed me and is accommodating me for a return to work I want.

If I knew my state pension here in the UK would be safe I would put my house up for sale and go back to the Netherlands. I have never felt so lost and alone. I wouldn't wish this upon my worst enemy!

C.V., The Netherlands

★★★

Just a few weeks before preparing to move from Paris to Frankfurt in 1995 as instructed by my husband's employer, we received a call to say that after all it would not be Germany but the UK. Dropped my German Language self-study books and rejoiced because I could speak English a bit better than German. I was quite happy too that the brand new channel tunnel would facilitate our visits to family in France. How exciting!

After 22 years of a busy and generally happy life, making sure we were doing all we could to fit in well here, working, raising family as everybody else, came the Referendum.

At first, I was optimistic and not worried as I could hear those in charge that there should be no change for those already here. So surely, 22 years of a stable life in the UK should be long enough to ensure we continue that way for many more years.

Suddenly it hits me! An EU colleague asked me if I had the same experience as her trying to get letters from our employer, and started to explain the process of PR to me. I had NO idea! A few days later another EU colleague told me of some of the other problems that people were having with applying for PR. I started to look into it for us, the more I unfolded it the more complicated it became and four months of stress followed.

I literally dropped everything else apart from work. I did not really see Christmas or my son's birthday, my mind was in Permanent-Residence-gear all the time. How exhausting! I thought naively that after receiving these blue cards I would relax, but this did not happen.

After a few weeks of hope following 'One Day Without Us' and witnessing debates in Parliament, it became clear that what I had initially heard in June about no change being on the table, this was no more on the agenda.

So now I wait, I wait and wait and prepare for more waiting – "as there is little you can do," as the local MP put it himself when I went to see him.

This is doing no good to my sanity but I'm trying to keep up with close family and work. My question is really now, how long will this wait last, when shall I reach my breaking point?

I hear about some of us who have made radically different decisions: moving away / getting citizenship. Well done you, you have made your mind! I admire you.

My mind is mal-functioning, due to Brexit, and no one seems to know how to repair the damage.... What a waste...

Juliette N., France

★★★

Some days feel to me as if something is poisoning the air. Only today I met an old acquaintance who asked how I was, what I was doing etc. Once the conversation turned to Brexit, he asked most worriedly, "Oh but it doesn't affect you, does it?" Well, of course it affects me, since I am European and so is my son. The history of my birth country has shown how easily a presumably civilised society can unleash demons that bring out the most barbaric instincts. I am aghast at the stuff I'm reading these days in the right wing press and in some comments I'm picking up online.

Only a few days ago the lovely term 'the enemy within' has been coined (more strong echoes of Weimar Germany here), referring – presumably – to all so-called Remainers, Brexit – opponents and immigrants. How can anybody possibly feel unaffected by it all in the current climate? One would have to be so thick-skinned. I think there is a huge amount of repression going on and I am wondering whether many people here feel deeply ashamed and embarrassed about this previously unimaginable situation, and are very uncomfortable in the company of people against whom much of this hatred is directed, wanting to turn away as a result, shut their eyes, not having to acknowledge.

But then, it is always human nature to have to steal glances at what you're trying to ignore.... the famous 'return of the repressed'. Not entirely sure whether this makes sense, but I feel that to assume that people's glances and reactions may not always be of a suspicious nature or because of racism, can make us perhaps feel a bit stronger. We've been part of this town for so long, we should carry ourselves proudly.

Gerlinda Rehberg, Germany

★★★

My husband is British. He is going to be 61 in April. I am French and I am going to be 55 in August. I have been in this country for over 32 years. I have worked since my arrival in England. I am a qualified teacher and I should receive my teaching pension in five years. My husband was a teacher and he is retired now. My worry is regarding my pensions, first of all, my teaching pension which I have paid for over 25 years and I should receive it in five years' time and, secondly, my state pension which I should receive in ten or 12 years. I have worked for 32 years, part-time, full-time. With Brexit, am I going still receive these pensions if I have to leave the country and, if my husband leaves with me, is he going to receive his pensions abroad? He has contributed for over 35 years and he has a part-time job at the moment. It is very worrying to not know how our future will be financially. We have five more years to finish paying for our house so we can't plan anything, especially if I have to leave. What penalties should I endure if I am staying?

P.R., France

★★★

I find it quite difficult to give this testimony but I shall do my best and choose to remain anonymous.

My sons and I returned to the UK in 1984. Both my sons were born in Italy, the youngest returned to live with his father and the eldest remained here in Scotland with me. Around 1991 my son had to return to Italy to complete his National Service and could well have done so remaining in the confines of Italy. My son had other ideas and chose to go to Somalia as part of the UN. He was in Mogadishu at the time of the 'Ground Bravo' incident. He came back to Italy and was decorated by the UN and the Italian MOD.

Unfortunately, he also came back with a drug habit and malaria. Since he had been inoculated in the army, doctors could not see nor find malaria until many months had passed and my son had liver problems. In the end it was detected and resolved. What was not resolved was his drug abuse and instead of getting my son help, his father threw him out of the house.

My son still had the intelligence to get himself back to Scotland and by the time he arrived he was in a very dark place. I noticed that he was psychologically ill, and for nearly five years, I fought to get him help. By the time he did get help, he was a full-blown schizophrenic. He has spent nearly five years in various institutions but eventually was finally discharged with a back-up team. This all took place 12 years ago.

To date, he has led an exemplary life. He had his own flat but because of my mobility and falls, we both decided to live together instead of living independently. Little did I ever consider how I would become dependent on my son. His help is given in all sorts of fashions; he is kind and caring and often completes tasks without even being asked.

He is very much aware of his illness and is regimented with his medication if he does not feel 100% he will pick up the phone and call his team. He has told me that he does not want to go to that dark place again, he would sooner die than let it happen.

So, this is the background. I have to find nearly £2k to get everything in order to apply for British citizenship for him. I am a disabled pensioner so I am not financially comfortable

Although I am British, the Home Office have told me my son is not eligible for British citizenship through descent.

If this is the case, then I fear there is a very strong possibility he could be deported.

I do not have property or savings but if ever my son is deported then I will leave this country to be with him. If he is on the streets, then so will I be. In any event, I could not remain here knowing that my son's life would be at risk.

About two years ago, my son and I were sitting admiring the view and I voiced that it was good to feel safe in a warm, clean environment and to have good neighbours. I also said that we had to be thankful to have gotten through so much and thankfully his mental health remained stable. He agreed with me and said that we were lucky to have defeated the odds.

That was until Brexit happened!

If it all sounds melodramatic, believe me the future does look grim and I am not playing to an audience.

I might have been to hell and back because of my son's illness but I know I have one very special person, who has a very big heart, who cares, and who is intelligent enough to understand his frail psychological condition. I just wonder if the Home Office will understand just as well.

M.T., British mother of an Italian national

★★★

It had never crossed my mind to come here before, but I felt I had no choice. I arrived in Great Britain four years ago when I was 34, after I was left unemployed. I chose Great Britain for its open culture, tolerance and multicultural environment. When I arrived in London, I didn't know anyone, didn't have any contact or job and only had little English.

I quickly found a room and I immediately loved the atmosphere of London, with its hectic, busy and crowded streets. I shared a flat with other people of different nationalities and really immersed myself in studying English but also looking for a job which I badly needed. After a long search, I was finally offered a position in a boutique in Oxford.

I moved to Oxford and found a room. For me it was a totally new job as I had never worked in retail before. I had many odd moments but met many people, made new friends, came across new customers and met a wonderful British man who became the man of my life. We found a place together, my job went from strength to strength, and I even got a pay rise.

When I remained pregnant with my first child, I had the support of my team from work and of lots of friends, especially my friend Stefi who was about to become a mother like me. When my son was born, my parents sold their house to help us buy our new home and my parents-in-law, or my 'parents-in-Love', as I call them, decided to help us too.

As soon as we moved to our new home with our five month-old baby, I realised that I was pregnant again. It was a surprise, both pleasant and shocking, to find myself expecting our second child soon after my new born baby, so I decided to resign from my job because I felt it was the proper thing to do after the company had given me so much. It didn't make sense to go to work for just another six weeks and be in maternity again. My salary wouldn't have covered the fees for the nursery of two toddlers anyway. We decided that I will be a full-time parent for the time being even if we had to face some sacrifices.

We married in April last year with a wonderful ceremony. We were so happy and in love – and then on the 23rd June, Brexit! With this nightmare my fairy tale has been left in tatters, my safe world destroyed.

From that day fear has slowly been creeping in my life. I feel stripped of my rights to be a citizen, a mother. I love my husband, my family, the life

I have built here. The European citizenship has given me the opportunity to choose, Brexit has taken it away.

I live in fear of being separated from my family and I tell myself this can't happen it won't happen. But the reality is that this government could decide to do it. Next year it will be five years since I moved here, but I do not think that I will be entitled to obtain permanent residency. I had no idea that there was a CSI requirement when I was in maternity leave. I discovered it just at the end of my maternity allowance and I don't think I can just present my maternity allow without the CSI. I am anxiously waiting for more information from the HO.

I am living in this limbo and it really hurts, not only for myself but for my children too.

Lia, Italy

★★★

I came to the UK in February 2010 from Poland. I already had a job contract signed through an employment agency while I was in Poland. I was going to work as Care Assistant in family run care home based in Berkshire, South East England.

Before I flew to London I did a lot of research about work in care plus I also had some essential knowledge about dementia and medical needs of elderly sufferers. I was a bit unprepared for the sad reality of private care home sector especially when it comes to employment's rights. I was hit hard but I continued.

I attended each and every personal and most of medical needs of my patients. I bathed them, fed them, changed their dressings, cleaned their stoma bags, held their hand when they were dying alone, washed them and dressed to look decent for funeral service. I had lovely colleagues but abusive, money-obsessed employers. I was fed up with how I was treated by my employers (like I was their belonging) so decided to try to get out from there. There was an opportunity to work for the Trade Union (to specialise in employment rights of care workers) which I took but it was not a permanent contract. It was 2014 and I got married in December to a Brit I met in March 2013.

In 2017 we were expecting our first child and were very excited. Soon after finding out we also learnt that there is a very high risk of our child being born with a genetic condition which can be potentially lethal and went through painful, invasive procedure followed by wait from hell to get an answer. I gave birth in July of that year and was lucky I lived and my son was healthy. Six months later my maternity pay ended and I remained a stay at home mum (we can't afford childcare cost in any way).

We had to move to a different county so I became very isolated because my whole family is in Poland and I have no friends at all where I live. I could not believe in the result of the Referendum but I can't say I was overly surprised. I knew very well from my care work how much xenophobia and racism exist among some people. Since then I observe in horror what's happening in this country. I feel like a second or even third class citizen.

My husband is British, my son is British. We can't agree on what we should do in the future. I have very little choice because my husband isn't keen on going abroad. I'm absolutely exhausted from constant discussion with him and constant worry. I know that probably no one will deport me but I see the very real threat that I will be unable to find any decent job in the future which is dangerous because we are very short of money. I don't qualify for any help and don't qualify for PR (I don't have five years' work in a row). I cannot afford CSI especially as I have a pre existing condition. I think that I paid well into this country by my work and five years of NI and tax contributions.

I'm worried to go out with my son into a public place because I have to speak in Polish so he understands and he's only 20 months. I'm worried to speak to my mum when in public. I avoid baby groups and was even concerned when going into Charity meeting because I knew that there will be a lot of people who voted Brexit for immigration reasons. I'm concerned about economical effect on our life in England because life in South East where my husband works is already very expensive. I just don't see the way going forward, for sure not at the moment.

Natalia Byer, Poland

★★★

As long as I can think I have loved history and cultures and languages. It is the very fabric of me, and I've never been afraid to talk to people from other countries and listen to their stories and be simultaneously amazed about how different yet similar their lives are.

I visited Great Britain for the first time when I was just a teenager. My marks in English were bad so I was sent to England to learn the language properly. I spent a wonderful summer both learning – together with teenagers from all over the world – about the use of the language as well as more of the history and culture of this island. The next year, my marks had much improved, I begged my parents to send me back here again and they complied. Another happy summer with fond and funny memories about 'the English'.

Fast forward 20 years, eight years ago. I was in my mid-thirties, unattached. Although I had a good job, I felt I wanted to have a change of scenery and now was the time. I've learnt a few more languages in the years between and could have easily ventured to Spain or other countries, but the British island has never lost its charm to me and I had spent many years of reading about English and Scottish history (and a bit of the other bits too). I was enthralled with the idea of living in this great country. So, I packed up and moved to Nottingham to find my personal Robin Hood and make my own fortune.

Sadly, it was just the time when a big recession had hit the country, so I tried unsuccessfully at first to find a job. The Jobcentre was anything but helpful and it took me some time to land my first job. Eventually I succeeded, yet only for a short time. The job I had was limited for a few months and then I was back in unemployment. However, this time it wasn't as bleak, as I was asked to work as a freelancer for the company I had just left, which couldn't afford me on a full-time basis. Although I went back to the Jobcentre for six months, I worked hard in those months not only to find a new job (which was still very difficult) but also to get ready for my own business. I went to plenty of seminars, secured a place in the New Enterprise Allowance scheme and eventually I was 'in business' – and I still am now. And I even found love. Success!!! Or so I'd hoped.

In the winter before Brexit I got very ill and that impacted my ability to work quite badly. In those many months I was unable to think, sleep, eat, work, live. My poor partner suffered with me but he never faltered, never (overly) despaired on me, he was and is my rock and I love him dearly for not giving up on me. In autumn 2016 I finally received my diagnosis of a rare chronic condition and was put on medication. My business, which was nearly hitting rock bottom, soared up again, my will to live, my ability to think, my life got quite well again.

But of course, in the middle of everything, Brexit crashed down on it. And with every month passing the prospects of my life here are hanging more and more by threads. My business is all about assisting companies with their sales on the European continent. But the public tender opportunities for UK businesses in Germany have dried up a bit as nobody wants to commit to a ten-year contract when things are so uncertain at the moment. Thus, my clients are in the waiting zone. That, however, puts my very existence at risk. I came to the UK full of hopes and certainty that I'll make the best of opportunities. In the last eight years I had to come to terms with the fact that recessions can hit even the most determined person.

Over the last 12 months I had to learn that speaking just the slightest of accents is enough to set people off, telling me to my face that Germans are Nazis – after I've spent my entire life feeling guilty for the very fact, that my birth country has a history full of atrocities. I've had to endure people complaining about those foreigners leeching the resources of this country, e.g. Job centres and NHS.

I had to come to terms with the fact that I am such a foreigner, who had bad luck with employment and now is in need of the security the NHS is offering to someone with a chronic illness, and cannot even make a decent living because my clients are afraid of what Brexit means for their businesses. I had to learn that my contributions into health and social insurances of two countries for over 30 years mean nothing when the UK leaves the EU. The rug has been truly pulled under my feet and I have to accept that all I had dreamed of can be taken away without me being allowed to have any say in that.

However, I cannot accept this. I am a human being, a good person, a person who believes in making connections across borders and language barriers. I strongly believe in the European project, albeit flawed and requiring improvements. It is a project of peace and community and togetherness. I don't want to feel an outcast simply because I've decided to move around a bit. I don't think it is right to tell me that I am a citizen of nowhere only because I've decided to be a European citizen, a citizen of the world.

My illness doesn't make me a bad person. My accent doesn't make me a bad person. My different upbringing doesn't make me a bad person.

So I trudge on, filling out an 85-page document, bringing 5 kg paper-work of proof, and can only but hope that this makes me worthy enough to live my life in a place of MY choosing with the British man I love.

Anonymous, Germany

★★★

Since the Referendum outcome last June the ice-cold shower sensation has almost never left me. The morning after the Referendum, my dearest neighbour approached our car and told us casually, "Nothing will change between us," and at the time it seemed quite reassuring. Thinking about it later though and reflecting on the very English attitude of 'It should be fine but eventually who really cares', I do not think it was that positive. Something along the lines of 'You will have to go through a lot of heart-ache but we will still be friends'. Actually our neighbourly relations have almost vanished and the other neighbours have become virtually invisible (we live in a small street and we know everybody, at least by sight).

From that moment, I have begun gradually to feel more and more fragile and at risk of being targeted and 'to feel a crock pot among iron pots'. I do not talk much, even at the grocery store I speak almost in a whisper. I do not talk on the phone outside the house, so that nobody can pick up my foreign accent and my Italian.

When I was in London, the city atmosphere was different. Here everything is more provincial, although this was actually the reason why we decided to move but now it has backfired. I often don't sleep at night, grind my teeth when I sleep and I have also had several crying spells, even at work, where everyone pretended not to notice. In a way that was better as I did not need to explain. At work I feel more and more like an outsider, despite those – almost compulsory – initiatives (which I personally find ridiculous) to gather together as a team. At work I feel a bit like an exotic animal. I had hoped that the novelty would pass after a while, but there is always someone who mocks me when I say a word which is not absolutely perfect. If before this was just annoying, now it has become painful.

My brother in law, who has had a British passport for a couple of years, keeps us informed on the recent developments and on the likely problems, and throws them on us just to make us worry and frankly this does not help. I think I have become an anxious person and I was never like this. I get worried easily and we have even started talking about a possible relocation. BUT WHERE TO?

We bought our house here two years ago, brought here all our stuff after selling in Italy and in any case we have lived here nearly five years. Would we really have the guts to pack up everything and start up again somewhere else? Or, will we have the courage to follow all the developments and look with suspicion at everyone's glance around us? Will we always live in fear? What will become of us later?

L.G., Italy

★★★

I have been living in North London since 1999 and despite a few hard moments, I'd say I always felt at home here. Work, friends, relationships: all normal stuff. Until last June. I have a young daughter with special needs and she needs her mummy. Now here's the problem. As we have no idea what rights, if any, we will retain after Brexit, the tension in my house is tangible and constant.

I have to do my PR application but I'm too busy with all other stuff and frankly I'm so pissed off I don't want to see papers. My husband has told me that if they deport me my baby cannot come with me because here she has a health support network. He's disgusted at the racist and xeno-phobic narrative and has no faith in the government.

We have been arguing a lot over my failure to produce all necessary documents for the application. I cannot help it if I no longer have all the flight confirma-tions of my travels for the last five years. I'm so stressed out I have a skin rash.

My daughter feeds on my anxiety and it's detrimental for her health. The thought that they will separate us fills me with a feeling worse than the fear of death. At least with death you know it's something that has to happen. Brexit should have never happened.

M.M., Italy

★★★

I have been in UK since July 2008 and I love UK. When I arrived here I started to work for the catering company through agency. It was sum-mer time and was very busy, we were pushed to work 16 hours a day, day shifts and night shifts without the day off. I did not mind as I loved the work, the only thing bothered me that my hands were so swollen as I was working on all the departments but mainly in prep area, where we were prepping the food. If I said that I would like day off I was told no and if I decided not turn up to work they would not give me work for a week or two as a punishment. So no choice there. At the winter time the company was not busy I was called to work for a few hours a week, I was lucky to have money to pay for rent and I had to go without food.

I found an extra job in Poundland, where they gave me a few hours here and there, still better than nothing. I did not leave the agency and come spring it was busy again. I was told to leave Poundland as they needed people or leave the agency as I could not pick and choose when I can work. So I left Poundland.

In 2009 I met my husband in the same catering company where I worked. He was a manager there. At the beginning we kept our relationship quiet as we knew people would be watching us, as soon as we came out with it I was told that I can't work in the same department as my husband cos he favourites me, which was not the case at all! There were managers and the staff too whose relatives were working in the same departments as them too and it was not a problem for them at all.

I got pregnant, pregnancy was difficult, I was very sick and swollen, but worked till the end. Then I got married to my British husband in 2010 and our baby boy was born, who I named after my brother who passed away when I was 16 years old, he was a year younger than me. The delivery was difficult and we were lucky for our boy to be with us. I also had postnatal depression. My husband helped me a lot and without him I would be lost. I went to work after my maternity in 2011. The agency was not busy and did not give proper hours to work, so I decided to look for another job.

During this period I found out I was pregnant again, we did not plan, but we were happy. I had morning sickness and we also found out my husband had cancer. He had his neck open, then 30 lots of radiotherapy and two lots of chemotherapy.

It was very difficult time and I could not continue to work as we did not cope very well. In 2011 our second son was born, we also were lucky that he survived. My husband was with me even he has his own battle to deal with. He was connected to the feeding machine while I was I labour. He was burnt and bless him he could not eat and that is why he was on the machine. After my maternity I was looking for a job for a month and then I started to work. My husband survived his battle with cancer, even though he was told he had less than 50% chance to survive. He went to work too. We shared the children while we were working as I was doing early shifts and he was doing lates.

As my older boy was growing I noticed something was not right with him. He was not speaking, he did not react to his name, just running around not eating... In 2013 he got diagnosed with autism, I was heart-broken, I cried and cried even at work, but was being careful people did not notice. In January 2014 I became a carer for my son.

A year later my younger son got diagnosed with autism at the same date just a year later than my older son. Yet again I was heartbroken. So since 2014 I have been a carer for my son. My husband became carer in 2015 too as it was difficult with both of them. Now with the Brexit nonsense I became aware that I needed CSI. I never knew about it before. As a carer to British children and as a wife to British husband I don't have any rights and I am not able to obtain my PR.

Even between 2008 and 2014 when I was working I don't qualify cos when we had the worst period of our lives I was on ESA (Employment and support allowance) for one or two months. I think it is unfair as I did not choose to be not well and my hubby to have cancer.

What also makes me upset is how easy it is for them to scrap people who have lived years in U.K. Like they are nothing... I am 28 years of age, I could start elsewhere, but not my children, they are happy here in UK. After 2 two weeks in Slovakia in summer they want to come back home, specially my older one as he has problems to cope with changes. Also my British hubby does not speak any other language than English.

I fear what is going to happen to my family. I HOPE THIS NIGHT-MARE WILL END SOON AND WE WILL BE LIVING WITHOUT FEAR YET AGAIN.

Ivana B., Slovakia

★★★

My story is as so many others. In 2004 I met and fell in love with my now British partner. We travelled back and forth for a year and then decided to take the plunge and live together. As he does not speak any Dutch it was obvious I would move to UK. In 2005 I moved here and was soooo excited... I always felt a strong bond with the UK after several holidays over the years. Even then it felt like coming home.

I made my life here, worked, paid taxes, bought a house, never used benefits or NHS as I am in good health. We have a good life, no debts and just a small mortgage.

As a European citizen, I never contemplated to become a British national. That would have meant losing my Dutch nationality and with that my Dutch state pension. Being 63, I depend on that pension. I worked in management consulting for diverse markets due to my language skills: Dutch, English, German and French. I never took someone else's job. As I try to explain my feelings and anxieties to my British friends and neighbours, it seems they do not understand them. Some random persons even told me to "go back home if I do not feel welcome anymore," and "you should have become British". It hurts and keeps me awake not knowing what will happen.

Being retired now, to apply for PR meant I had to take out CSI. We all came here to the UK in good faith, contributed to the economy, and never expected to be treated like second class citizens. If it comes to the point that I will not be able to stay and have to go back to the Netherlands, what happens to my partner? He does not manage the languages to be able to get a job. We'd have to sell our house, leave our life, family and friends. It is also very troubling for my mother-in-law who is 83, as we are her only family living close.

The uncertainty has taken a great toll on our lives, ever since the outcome of the Referendum. Neither of us can understand why the government is unable to give us the right to stay NOW. The British government is using us, people, lives, family and friends as bargaining chips. Moreover, it's not just us, EU citizens in the UK, but also all British expats, scattered all over Europe. For me, the way we are used is so beyond comprehension. You never expect this to happen in a democratic nation like the UK. I am very angry, sad, anxious, gutted. The country I love and the people I love are no more... In just a few months it's all changed. The worst is that many people do not understand how we feel, so we can't get support from anyone other than fellow EU citizens.

Monique Bredius, The Netherlands

PART IV

"This is MY LIFE they are messing with,
MY HOME and MY FAMILY."

When I first arrived here in 1985, I still needed to register with the Home Office, which I did, and got my temporary residency permit. Then, in the next 18 months or so, the rules changed, and I no longer needed to apply for permanent residency. As an EU citizen, I was automatically granted permanent residency, but, here's the kicker, the Home Office didn't bother sending out permanent permits, because it was no longer necessary to have one. With me so far?

I have toyed with the idea of getting British nationality over the years, sure, but, well, it was never urgent, it was expensive, and I always had other things more important to do, and after all, what did it matter? I married my British love, our kids were British, we have a mortgage and one day, our house will be ours outright, and I have never been one to bother with nationalism, and flags, so what if I kept my passport rather than getting a British one, it was not important.

Fast forward to now. Post Brexit, not being allowed to have a say in the matter despite living here for over 30 years galled me hugely, and spurred me into action, and I decided to go for it, apply for British citizenship. It shouldn't be a big deal, right?

Ah ah ah (hollow laugh). Turns out that, behind the scenes, over the last few years, the goalposts have been moved.

For starters, since 2015, in order to gain citizenship, you MUST have permanent residency; despite the fact that you haven't needed it since 1986 or so. They quietly reinstated those rules for EU citizens, but didn't tell us.

Ok, so I'll apply for PR, shouldn't be a big deal, right? I mean, I have been here over 30 years, paying taxes, National Insurance, I have bank accounts, a mortgage, a permanent address, kids, a British husband etc...

Ah. Well, the forms are 85 pages long. 85 pages long. Question after question after question, asking you to list every single time you have been in and out of the country (WHY?), where you've been, for how long... It wants bank statements, it wants to know every bit of your life detailed since you've been here. P60, P45, Piss off! How have you been supporting yourself? Can you support yourself?

And, here's the absolute kicker of them all: Since 2005, yes, you read that right, 2005, every EU citizen resident in my kind of situation* in the UK MUST have private Comprehensive Health Insurance. Say what, I hear you say? Yep, that's right. First I've heard about it. I also fail to understand how and why, when the whole point of reciprocal agreements is that I can use the local health services, and what's more, I have done so since 1985 without any issues.

I can also tell you that no one, but absolutely no one in my situation, EU residents in the UK, knew about it either. No one was ever told. Not those who, like me, have been here before the requirement came in 2005, no one who settled in the UK after 2005. It is buried somewhere in the paperwork, and doesn't get pointed out or stated at any point.

And guess what, apparently, if you haven't fulfilled these criteria you weren't aware of, you cannot get PR, and if you can't get PR, you can't get British nationality. Ta-DA!

So there you go. As we speak, people like me are being turned away, are being refused what they thought would be a fairly easy piece of paper to obtain, for failing to have something they didn't know they were supposed to have, and which of course cannot be got retroactively. What's more, the same people, people like me, who never questioned their right to be here, are being told they need to make arrangements to leave the country, I kid you not.

There are three millions of us. Three MILLION EU citizens who have settled in the UK, for work, for love, for whatever reason, and who suddenly do not know what the future holds for them. Let me tell you that it is terrifying.

*My kind of situation: people not having five years of continual employment, carers, stay at home parents, sick or disabled people, etc, etc. Please note that even if you have a British partner/husband who has been earning enough to support the family, it does not count.

Marie L. Pace, France

★★★

I grew up in Milan. I was fortunate enough to go to an international school. There I was immersed in a British education system with softly spoken native English teachers who taught me British values. I moved to the UK in 1991 to get a degree in and I fell in love with London at a time when Italy was under Berlusconi, when politics was polarised and Italians very divided. I felt at home there as I finally felt I could be myself.

After completing my studies between London and Brighton, I moved to Brussels where I got my first job at the heart of the EU. But I badly missed the UK, which I left on the day Diana died and just before Labour won the election. I longed to be back in London, where most of my friends lived. Finally, I moved back with my boyfriend in 2001. I got married and had three children. I always felt at home in an ever more cosmopolitan London… at least until that dreaded 24th June. In the run up to the Referendum my husband and I campaigned in the streets, we organised a local event to teach our neighbours about the EU and we hoped that Brits would see sense in the end. I felt as if someone had died on that terrible day. I felt my idyllic image of Britain had been shattered and everyone was against me and my family. I listened incessantly to the radio and watched the news non-stop to try to make sense of what was happening to the country I had chosen as my own. Then, I wished things would go so horribly wrong for the UK that they would have to change their mind – and then I felt really bad for thinking that. It was an emotional rollercoaster.

Nine months on and I am actively campaigning locally, and I spend all my free time working with the pressure group the3million standing up for our rights. I can't decide whether to stick it to the government by standing firm or rather by leaving to take my kids back to 'Europe' so that they can grow up feeling proud of being European. Who knows what the future holds? All I know is we must make our voices heard and if we do leave we won't do so quietly.

Costanza de Toma, Italy

★★★

I still remember how excited and nervous I was when Austria held a referendum on joining the EU in 1994, and how happy I was when the result was Yes. I was 18 then and was allowed to vote for the first time. My life since then has been shaped by the EU and the possibilities it offered, and I feel very lucky that I had the chance to make the most of these opportunities, and I feel sad for young people today that they won't get that chance. I got a translation degree, I did an Erasmus exchange year in Edinburgh, and in 2006, after being made redundant from my job in Vienna, I decided to live and work in England. I ended up in Norwich, and after over ten years, I'm still here!

Ever since I was little, I was fascinated by the English language – I remember wanting to be able to read the novels in English my mum (an English teacher) had lying around. Britain always appeared to me as this open, tolerant, friendly country, but that illusion has been thoroughly shattered.

My original plan was to just work here for a few years, but over the years I've grown roots here, and I call Norwich my home now. Two years ago, I met my

English boyfriend and life is good – apart from Brexit, that is. I'm one of the lucky ones – I should qualify for permanent residency. I haven't had the mental energy to tackle this task yet, especially since I have to sort out the issue of having had two different national insurance numbers due to a misunderstanding.

I'm also lucky in that I haven't had any direct problems with post-Brexit hostility or racism. But Brexit still was a kick in the teeth, I feel passionately about the European project, and to see it rejected on the base of venomous lies and blatant ignorance was painful to see. Europe is my home. I would never consider taking British citizenship, because it would mean giving up my Austrian citizenship (I'm not feeling particularly patriotic but I would never give up my EU citizenship).

Suddenly being part of a group of people who are considered 'undesirable' in this country has been both upsetting and humbling – as somebody from a well off western European country it's a new experience, and it made me even more aware of the plight of refugees and immigrants in the world.

I'm at a stage in my life where it would be nice to settle down permanently, but any long-term plans have been put on hold. Going back to Vienna would be an easy way out, but I like my life in Norwich, and even though my partner says he'd come with me if things here got really bad, I don't know how easy it would be for him as he only speaks a little High School German. Ten years ago, I made a decision in good faith, and I I'm upset and angry that my life is now in limbo.

Elisabeth, Austria

★★★

I took up an internship as a vet in England in 2000, followed by a residency in Scotland. The plan was to specialise and go back home to Germany. However, life happens and I met my English husband, fell in love, stayed, had kids and built my life in the UK. I was in love with my new home and proud of the tolerance that prevailed in my beautiful host country.

Then the Referendum happened. Don't even get me started on the thick lies told by both sides of the campaign and the failure of Remain to highlight the benefits of the EU to the UK. Spilt milk!

Although everyone thought the Referendum was a done deal and Remain would surely win, all I could see even in our area, which is very much well off, well educated, white middle class, were 'Leave' signs, which was very worrying. My husband was so sure that it would not be an issue that he needed a lot of persuasion to even go and cast his vote. For the whole family, as the kids were too young and I had no voice and felt powerless.

I saw the first results come in that evening and was convinced it had gone the wrong way. Unfortunately I was right. In the morning after I woke up to what felt like a different country. I felt shocked, unwelcome, unwanted, a sense of grief and betrayal and frankly scared! For myself, my family – and this country as a whole. There is so much negativity and strong bitter feelings on both sides. One of the mums in school apologised to me the day after but no one could understand the depth of my grief. I was distraught and collapsed in a heap of crying, sobbing doom a few times. "It will be alright." "You should be ok." "No-one will deport YOU!" Even some UKIP supporters, who were my clients prior to the Referendum attested to me that I was the kind of immigrant that was welcome in the UK. And I had never even thought of myself as an immigrant. And why should I be treated differently to other people who had made their lives in the UK, in good faith and based on the same assumptions as I had? Why should there be more and less desirable immigrants?

My parents in law voted out. We called them the next day, they told us and said: "We thought you were one of us!" I thought so, too, up until the 24th June...

Why did no one run a campaign introducing some of the different scenarios of EU nationals who had come to the UK and contribute to this country? Making it personal, introducing mixed EU families, explaining their stories. Why did they not debunk the myths with facts? Why did they not explain the vast benefits of the EU to everyone? Of course, the EU is not perfect. That doesn't mean that they are responsible for the chronic underfunding of the NHS, schools, prisons, infrastructure and other public services that have happened over the past many years. I am not angry with all the people who voted out. Just the ones who did it for the wrong reasons. And I am angry with people who now say that they did have all the right information and voted out because of it. I am also VERY angry with campaigners, who should have known better as it is their job, and who clearly got behind the Leave campaign for personal gain and nothing else.

I am sure many who did vote out, did so with the best interest of the UK at heart. Although I fail to be convinced of the positives of Brexit for the country, this is the situation we find ourselves in. Whichever way you voted in the Referendum, the uncertainty following the result has caused distress for many people. Non-UK EU citizens in particular, and this needs to be addressed.

Being a German national, some of the policies coming out of Westminster these days remind me of a very dark chapter of the history of my own country, e.g. the proposal to make businesses compile a list of foreign employees. The rise of hate crimes is also very disturbing. And some politicians seem content that they can still use the immigrants and the EU as their scapegoat at the moment... What will they do if the UK does indeed exit and the EU cannot be blamed anymore?

Eight months after the Referendum, it remains unclear what Brexit will mean to us EU nationals and indeed this country. The PM promises she will make a success of leaving the EU. I am not convinced that that is possible and that the damage can only be contained, if EU nationals currently in the UK who contribute to vital services, e.g. veterinary professionals and NHS staff, are on her side. At the moment she seems to do little to achieve this or even to try.

I feel I have earned the right to have a British passport, as I have lived here for such a long time and have contributed in many ways. I do not want anymore to be in the UK and not even have a say in an election again. However, I don't want to apply and pay the money, if I will then have to decide which nationality to keep if Brexit does go through. German law currently only allows dual nationality if the second country is an EU country. And I will NEVER give up being German. In recent years I have been quite proud of my nationality. Quite a surprising and unusual feeling for me as I grew up being ashamed of our past. I guess on the whole we have learned from it. Never to be repeated! Therefore I can still hear voices from stories I read about Nazi Germany with people asking: "Why didn't you do anything? Why didn't you leave when you still could?" So I am sometimes asking myself, why I should stay here? But then I guess life is never that simple and you can just up sticks and go. Not with a family and deep roots that come with that.

I am not a political person. However, this issue has such wide reaching consequences for me and my family that my little girl and I went on the March to Parliament. She made me very proud when she made a poster we took to the march. My husband was worried and said we should be careful as he feared that right wing activist may harass us. We went with a Dutch friend and her little girl and it was great to see so many come out for this issue. People from all walks of life who took the time to travel to London and march against this madness. On the way back we had some lovely chats with people who were very supportive and it felt like we had done something rather than surfing Facebook pages and getting depressed about the dark future that potentially awaits us. It was a bit disappointing that the media largely ignored the march.

I hope so much that a second referendum with the terms of Brexit will be won on facts rather than fables.

Ariane Watts, Germany

★★★

This situation is crazy! The way things stand at present is that it is easier to get my Border Collie dog into Europe with a pet passport than to keep my Dutch husband in this country, and he has lived here for over 40 years!

He wants to stay in the UK. We want him to stay in the UK. Our family is here – our daughter, son-in-law and two grandchildren. He has worked in the British Library and carries out honorary work at Cambridge University Library. He has a UK Civil Service pension and state pensions from the UK and Holland. We cannot apply for PR as he cannot get CSI due to pre-existing medical conditions. He has published a great deal on the positive and historical impact of immigration in the UK. A few years ago he took part in a Channel4 series called Bloody Foreigners about how the Dutch were originally blamed, falsely, for starting the Great Fire of London.

Surely this cannot really be happening in this caring, compassionate and open-minded United Kingdom?

Anna H., a UK citizen married to a Dutch national who has lived in this country for over 40 years

★★★

Autumn 1974: A little seed that was planted during the summer that is starting to find its way to my heart. I am 13 years old.

Autumn 1977: That's it, I know, I just know. Live in England is what I want to do at some point but the sooner the better. Many things feed off and nurture this little seed: Films (Le Taxi Mauve, Barry Lyndon, Sunday Bloody Sunday, The Avengers (always, since childhood), The Prisoner etc.), a voracious appetite for Thackeray, Dickens, Hardy, Trollope and the modern classics.... A complete mishmash of new sounds I bring home via Mike Oldfield, the Rubettes (yes, them!), Queen... combined with religious listening to the weekly charts on radio; and I know, I just know.

Comes 1983 and my first long stay in the UK, teaching for a year. Those months were hard and unhappy overall. Still, the time that followed back in France showed me how much I missed the UK and confirmed my wish, my need, to live here. Roll on the end of 1986 and I move here to stay. The rest is my history.

So how do you explain how or why one is attracted to a language, a country, a culture? Ironically, it's an intangible 'je ne sais quoi' that I knew I should follow, and follow I did. I studied English at uni and my MA was on 18th century England, followed by a specialist post grad degree in English. I certainly was not and still am not rejecting my French heritage, but I could not go on living in France. It was impossible. I was suffocating.

For 30 years now, England, the UK, has been my home. My friends are my family and most also live here. The UK is where I have now spent all my adult life, worked, studied for an MPhil in an English University, loved, unloved, made plans, cried and been happy... I'm short lived.

I am a European, true and true. I was born and brought up in Picardy where folks have experienced three wars in the space of seventy years. This creates a very grounded sense of what Europe can be and do. My grandfather was involved in both the First and the Second World War and entirely embraced the European project which he always supported it in spite of its failings. When I emptied their house in 1993, I found over 300 empty jam jars they had kept from the last war. I kept a couple of the lids; one says "1l melted butter, 17 July 1943". This is a poignant reminder of how fragile life can be. They lived the next 45 years convinced there would be another war and that they should be ready for it. Hence the jars. Europe brought peace instead.

On the morning after the Referendum, I felt like someone had pulled the rug from under my life. Since then I have felt that something had irremediably changed. For someone who'd spent her life fighting the odds, this was one odd too many. I spent days and days inconsolable.

A couple of weeks after the Referendum, I realised that in order to survive, apathy just was not an option. I had to act, I had to do something. Shortly after, the 3million group was born and the rest is the3million's history. I have invested every single waking hour in this fight (and most of my nights re-enact my waking hours in funny ways!) but I still do not know whether I will be allowed to stay in the UK. Whenever I consider all my options, including moving to another EU country or trying France again, I can feel my heart tear to bits. Home is here! How do you disentangle from thirty years of life? My life is not a trade deal to be negotiated, despite what some would have you believe... And yet, my funny life story means the Home Office probably won't like it if and when I do apply for the dreaded PR certificate. My chances of getting it are slim. My employment history has been rocky due to life circumstances, not the sort of ideal applicant the Home Office is looking for.

Friends have been supportive, including leave supporters in various degrees of blissful denial of the facts. I am hanging on in there but I have no clue what tomorrow is made of. I want to do a 'Bobby Ewing' and wake up from what surely is a dreadful nightmare of ginormous proportions. Often I just feel like I'm acting out the words of Steve Smith's poem: Not waving but drowning. And yet, every day I keep trying. How long for, I don't know. All I know is that this whole sorry and insane mess has-to-stop.

Anne-Laure Donskoy, France

★★★

I was on my way to work a few months ago when I received a call from my sister in Greece informing me that my father, who was terminally ill with cancer, had died that morning after a difficult night in the hospital. I had already booked tickets to fly the next morning in the hope to see him one last time while he was still alive but sadly it was too late for that. I had to overcome the feeling of helplessness and keep my calm to make arrangements for the funeral so I had to use the limited time I had until I got to work for that. I was on the phone to my family speaking in Greek arranging the details and still on the Overground when the British person sitting opposite me started staring at me. I failed to notice until it was rather obvious, at which point he said to me – as he was getting up and walking towards the doors – "We voted you lot out. Go back to Poland." He said that and got off the train immediately. I would have confronted him but I was too shocked for that. I often think about that day and no matter how hard I try I just can't seem to find the words to describe how traumatic it felt. It burnt a hole in my heart, I'm still angry, and I feel this is a legitimate feeling.

N.M., Greece

★★★

I am a French resident living in Yorkshire and I would like to obtain a permanent residence certification/card (PR), currently mandatory to become a UK citizen. However, the current system of PR discriminates against many groups of EU residents. The comprehensive sickness insurance (CSI) as PR requirement for EU students, homemakers or self-sufficient applicants was never made clear to anyone moving to the UK from Europe. It is only now that the Home Office has started to enforce this rule which penalises stay-at-home parents and non-working EU citizens married to working British partners. At the time, I made the decision to stop working as a teacher to look after my two children and to go to university to study in view of changing career, I was not made aware of this requirement; being self-sufficient, I would have happily paid for CSI.

I have obtained a training contract in a national law firm starting in 2018, after gaining work experience in law firms and working as a volunteer student advisor and administrator for my university legal advice clinic, helping people with housing issues. I have worked as a teacher for five years but not for five consecutive years, therefore my working time cannot be used for my qualifying period.

I studied at university for seven years since coming to this country in 1999: I completed a Postgraduate Certificate in Education between my teaching years; then during my pregnancies, I did a Masters in International Education Management (Distinction); and in the last four years, while being a full-time mum, I have studied a Postgraduate Diploma in Law (Commendation) and this year, I am finishing my Postgraduate Legal Practice Course and Masters in Law and Business Management.

I have been married to my English husband for nearly 15 years and I am aiming to work in England until I retire. I have never claimed benefits and I am looking forward to starting my new career as a commercial lawyer. I would like to know what the government intends to do to retain people in my situation who make a valuable contribution to society.

C.B., France

★★★

My upbringing was, in some respects, quite conservative and narrow. Growing up in a Somerset village in the 1970s, my exposure to people from other European countries was non-existent. Thankfully, however, in my late teens I was able to go to university, which gave me the chance of meeting students from around the world, and this was literally a life defining experience. Many of this group of exotic (at least from my perspective) young people were from other parts of Europe. I soon realised that their presence here was courtesy of an EU exchange programme – it was actually the embryonic stage of the Erasmus scheme – and I was immediately impressed by the fantastic possibilities it was providing for so many people across Europe (not least my British contemporaries).

For me this encounter was life changing as, among other things, it allowed me to meet my future wife (then an exchange student from France). After our studies, settling down into a life in Britain, it seemed that we were a real part of the EU experiment. We were living proof that national borders were no longer such a hindrance to travel, studies, careers, marriages or families. What progress!

Unfortunately, that all seems a long time ago now, and it appears that the changes currently afoot are likely to turn the whole situation on its head. We had confidence that the invitation my wife had received, to come to Britain to study, to marry and to settle, was for good, not just a temporary pass that could be revoked at any time. However, after 30 years in the UK, and 27 of them married to me, a British citizen, suddenly her future in this country is being put in doubt. Being a writer, my wife's income has always been irregular, and the tax she has paid has largely been in France. Now we understand that the Home Office classes someone in this position as 'self-sufficient' – something my wife has never been made aware of in all her time in this country. Moreover, someone in that situation apparently needs to sign up to CSI, to cover all of their health needs (even though in the UK health insurance providers do not cover the simplest of needs such as GP or A&E visits). The fact that my wife's private health cover, which she has had for years, would not be considered as 'comprehensive' by the Home Office means that Permanent Residency is almost certainly out of reach at this time.

So, what does this all mean for us as an EU couple? Unless a specific agreement is reached in the negotiations between the UK and other member states, it may be the case that my wife will not be granted leave to remain in the UK in the future. The message would be 'go back home' (this so called 'home' being a country in which my wife has never lived as an adult). And what about me? This action would be revoking my own right to marry and live with my French wife in the UK. But Brexit will also be simultaneously stripping me of my right to work and settle elsewhere in the EU. Consequently, even if my wife were to relocate to France it would be increasingly difficult for me to follow her, as my current citizenship of 28 countries is shortly to be downgraded to just one!

I am fully aware that these sorts of difficulties (and countless other variations) are being faced by a huge number of individuals, couples and families at the moment. I am angry that all of these personal tragedies are being ignored by our government, the message being that individual lives do not matter when political ambition is at stake. I am angry having to deal with the immediate fallout of the UK's pursuit of Brexit, but I am also very angry on behalf of the future generations of British children who will not be presented with the same opportunities as we were.

For all youngsters the whole point of growing up is to discover yourself and the world, to expand your horizons and to explore the opportunities that come your way. Everything in a young life should be about progress, about looking forward to the next stage. But how can youngsters look forward if they are growing up in a country that is determined only to look backwards? We are currently bombarded by talk of Britain's past, ranging from stories of the British Empire and Commonwealth to the nostalgia of the imperial measurement system! We are led to believe that shutting down our borders and restricting movement is the future. There are even some who are determined to promote an atmosphere of renewed distrust, animosity and even hatred of our European neighbours. How can such constraints and toxic feelings motivate youngsters? As I said above, I recognise how lucky I was to live through decades of hope, positivity and real progress, but why was this window of opportunity so short? Why should it be denied to our children and grandchildren?

And then I also think of my parents. Like me, they too had had very little opportunity to meet people from other European countries. However, my marrying a French wife also gave my parents the chance to befriend a similar family to theirs, but from the other side of the Channel (something that would never have happened otherwise). I know that this has been a really fulfilling and enriching experience for them, even though they spoke very little of each other's languages! For me, that's what the EU is all about: building a network of countless peaceful and loving relationships between all sorts of people, whether it is friends, couples, extended families or work colleagues. It is extremely clear to see how beneficial the building of such relationships is on an individual basis and how, by extension, this process can result in an extremely strong bond between whole populations, so long as it is given time to develop.

Miles, UK

★★★

This occurred on Saturday March 11th 2017. It is regarding an unnecessary comment made to me by a deliveryman. On signing for the parcel he checked to see if I was the person whose name is on the parcel, so as I signed I pronounced my name. Response: "Oh so you're one of them."

On that note he turned around and left. Needless to say it somewhat soured my Saturday morning and I decided to contact both the delivery company and the company I bought the item from. Both were quick to respond and apologise, promising investigations etc. but it still does not feel right. I am going back to them asking what measures have they in place to try stop this from happening and what about their employees who are not British citizens?

I have lived and worked here for 28 years with a NL/CH heritage and have an adult son who was born here.

Rachel Pauli, The Netherlands/Switzerland

★★★

When I arrived for a summer job in London in 2000, it was not my first time in the city; I had visited twice before and had loved it. That summer, I made some friends, amongst them my neighbour and future husband. For two years we were in a long-distance relationship while I finished my master's and professional qualification in France.

In 2002, I moved to London, worked in a school for disabled children as a learning support assistant. My then boyfriend was writing his PhD thesis and had no money left in his grant so my wages supported both of us. Thankfully, after eight months he secured a post-doctoral research job at the university. I ended up working at that university's library, doing various jobs. I also studied for a graduate diploma as I found my French qualifications were worthless here.

In 2007, we got married; the year after, as my husband's contract was coming to an end, he was awarded a fellowship funded by the EU to work as a researcher in a Swedish university. We moved to Sweden and our daughter was born there. In 2011, we decided to move back to the UK. I was a stay at home mother for a while, and after our daughter started pre-school, I found my current job at another academic library.

After the Referendum, I thought of moving to France, but then changed my mind and decided to wait and see, as I know how hard it is to start a life from scratch. Recently I decided to apply for PR and my world fell apart: according to the Home Office, I 'don't qualify for PR because I did not exercise [my] treaty rights for five consecutive years'. This is because I left the UK for more than two years, and I lacked CSI when I was a stay at home mother (though I had never ever heard of it).

Since then my feelings change daily from anger to despair. Being the wife and the mother of British citizens counts for nothing, having lived here for more than 12 years in total counts for nothing; there are three millions of us and we count for nothing, we are just pawns in a political game.

Vanessa, France

★★★

I had difficulties in obtaining the PR. I have been living in the UK for ten years now and my PR application was denied twice by the Home Office. The evidence I provided for self-employment included tax returns for six years, NI for ten years. I've been a registered resident (with the blue card) from 2009. I have a one year old son who is a British citizen with a British passport.

The reason given to be by the home office was that they could not establish that I was residing in the UK.

Teodor Lingurar, Romania

★★★

I came here to study, but then life just happened to get in the way of my other plans and I got stuck. It's easily done in an amazing city like Liverpool and I can think of worse places to settle.

In 1988, I moved to London to study A-levels at a private college, but London being the expensive city it is, the maintenance I received from my father only barely covered the rent for a small room and therefore I worked in a bar for minimum wage, paid tax and made National Insurance contributions, alongside bringing approximately £15,000 into the country in school fees and maintenance during those two years.

Then I had a gap year, which I spent working in Germany to save up money to support myself while studying, before I started University in Liverpool in 1991. Instead of working during term time, I chose instead to work like crazy in Germany during the holidays and bring all the money I had earned into the UK, amounting to approximately another £20,000 during my undergraduate degree. The wonderfully resilient Scousers were welcoming and thankful for the contribution made by students to the local economy. After graduating with a BA, I started research work on a PhD, but part time as I couldn't afford the full-time fees. My father supported me with tuition fees, but as he was retiring he could no longer give me maintenance so I looked for work locally and went to the Jobcentre. After claiming Jobseeker's Allowance for five months, I got a part time job teaching A-Level German at a local college.

In 1996 my mother died very suddenly and I started developing serious health issues which got worse and in 1999 I had to drop out of my PhD due to ill health. In 2000 I fell in love with a Scotsman and my father died. There was no way I could move to Scotland while grieving and there was nothing left in Germany for me to move back to, so the Scotsman moved to Merseyside to be with me. By now I had started working as a self-employed tutor as I simply couldn't find a full-time job and wasn't really well enough to work full-time anyway. We were married in 2003, split up in 2005, then got back together and had two kids, while also supporting each other through bereavements, miscarriage, fertility treatment, ill health and the trials of self-employment and entrepreneurship.

We don't have any wider family support here, it's just hubby and me – there are no aunties, grannies etc. – so raising two kids and just surviving already takes all the energy we have. My daughter is a gifted gymnast, hoping to compete at the 2024 Olympics, but it doesn't look like she will be representing Team GB, maybe she will make Scotland proud instead. I have looked at the timeline for Brexit and it is due to be complete six months before my daughter starts secondary school so, even though she is a British citizen, she will not be able to join her friends at the specialist Music and Mathematics academy I have had in mind for her ever since she started school in 2012.

On the morning of the 24th June, when I saw the Referendum result, I said in a moment of shock, "That's it, we're leaving!" and my little girls aged nine and six, burst into tears. They are embedded in this community and do not want to leave! When my older daughter got to school, her best friend (whose mother was terminally ill at the time and has since died) was in tears at the thought that we might be moving away. Wherever we go, we will be hoping for somewhere that can meet our children's needs academically as well as in sport, which means that there are many more criteria to meet than if I were on my own! Looking for work abroad (never mind schools and language lessons, gymnastics coaches, ballet and violin teachers – oh and accommodation! You know a roof over one's head is a nice thing to have…)

On the rare occasions when we visit Germany, my cousin jokingly refers to us as the refugee children, because in researching and refurbishing the old house he inherited, he discovered that after the war it was home to 46 refugees (with three toilets). Oh the irony! At this rate we really will be refugees!

Our only hope now is for an independent Scotland, although the climate is poison for my health and I am likely to be permanently disabled and would rather move to Greece, but my husband and children only speak

English and he has no confidence that he would be able to find work since he doesn't really have any qualifications to speak of and is developing health problems as well now. We're not really young enough to start again from scratch. We have no savings, no assets and a big pile of debt, so at the moment we couldn't even afford an airfare to get out of here.

You can imagine that in this situation there is just no energy or headspace left for 90-page forms to apply for PR (which is a moot point as I refuse, categorically and on principle, to apply for something that I was told I had acquired automatically once I had been here for eight years – instead of five, because I was here for education). Not to mention that I would be likely to have any PR application rejected (not that I am ever going to make one), as nobody mentioned CSI, so where would I find proof that I had private health insurance in Germany until 2000? By which time, incidentally, I had been here for 12 years – but some of them with a non-domiciled status as there are more than 90 days per year in which I worked abroad in order to pay for studying here! There is also no energy for campaigning.

I wonder whether I am more sensitive to the way in which the country under this government is slipping further and further to the right, because I come from Germany and was raised with the collective guilt over WW2 and the holocaust. When people ask me where I am from, I never refer to myself as German, I always say that I am from Germany – it is only a fine distinction, but a very important one to me. And yet, living in the UK, i.e. a country other than the one I grew up in – has certainly broadened my horizons. I have questioned what it means to have those negative parts to my history and I have discovered that there are also things to be proud of with the label 'German' (for me that's Goethe, Brecht and Beethoven just as examples). My friend described it perfectly once: "When people ask you where you are from and you answer, 'Germany,' there is a moment, a short silence, and in that moment I imagine that they immediately think of the Holocaust, the Second World War and the Nazi regime."

If you never leave the country you grew up in, you simply do not have these moments. You are never challenged to evaluate what is associated with the history of your country. Of course, wherever we go, we will survive. We will make a new life for ourselves. In the long run, the girls' lives will be enriched by exposure to different cultures, even if leaving and change hurts in the short term.

But right here, right now, I am angry and bitter! One of my in-laws voted leave and we do not know whether it was my mother-in-law or her husband. This has created a sense of betrayal within our own family and I feel uncertain about how to speak to them. Whilst I have had some very interesting debates with friends who planned to vote leave before the Referendum and there was a clear agreement that we both wanted what is best for this country but just disagreed on what that is, I have since then also had online abuse hurled at me for being 'a lefty wanker', 'commie bastard', 'Johnny Foreigner' and a 'Remoaner'.

That bitterness is likely to stay with me forever. It is not only about the Referendum result, but also about the behaviour of the government in the aftermath. The 'hard Brexit' that they are steering for, the discovery that since 2012 being married to a British citizen counts for nothing in getting citizenship, that the CSI rule was quietly introduced and is now being enforced without any information being made available on this (even the DWP disagrees with the Home Office on how the rule should be interpreted), the new rules brought into effect in February 2017, which put in place the mechanisms to deport people in my situation, the betrayal by the House of Commons in rejecting the amendments to the Brexit bill made by the Lords, the way in which doctors, nurses and employers are being made responsible to check people have a right to rent or a right to be here… I'm not even mentioning that suddenly my children are asked in the playground where their mum is from.

During my time in the UK, two thirds of my life, I have contributed to my local community by teaching first aid with the British Red Cross, got very involved in the PTA in my children's school, and was a Volunteer Games Maker at the Olympic and Paralympic Games in London 2012. I have saved a life, volunteered in school: teaching children to read when they had fallen behind, run a community group providing childcare in the form of educational experiences based on play and organised a family festivals benefitting the local community….and now?

Now all I have accomplished seems to be immaterial as I am just a bargaining chip. This is MY LIFE they are messing with, MY HOME and MY FAMILY.

Gertrud Wiethölter, Germany

★★★

My struggle with Brexit is both on an identity level and on a relationship level. It has brought up a lot of questions in terms of where home is, if I belong anywhere and whether I want to continue supporting a country that sees me as 'other'. I suddenly feel that I have to stand in line and prove myself, that I am good enough to be here.

My instinct is to profess to all the great things I have done for this country but this is the trap I endeavour to avoid, one of being apologetic about my rights here. On a relationship level, my British boyfriend voted Leave. He didn't discuss it with me in detail as he knew I opposed to it. When I woke up next to him on the 24th of June I couldn't believe what was happening. I left him but went back to him one month later. Nine months on and there are deep wounds in our relationship, admittedly there were issues to start with. I am still governed by feelings of betrayal and a sense of division within my relationship. Him and many others couldn't have predicted the layers of and the ripple effects of Brexit. He suspected that a Leave vote would only mean EU reform not an exit. He would vote differently now. But the damage is largely done as I feel that with his vote he jeopardised my sense of wellbeing and minimised my life's trajectory (I am here and have met him and my best friends because of freedom of movement). I am currently experiencing multiple strange feelings, I am worried about the feelings of division and separation this elicits in many of us. Feelings of anger and loss too. Time is needed to move to a new space emotionally and practically for us Europeans.

Anonymous, Greece

★★★

I fell in love with a Scotsman living in the Midlands. He healed me from years of abuse in France. This country saw me maturing and I was really keen to do everything I could to be useful to my new community.

So I'm volunteering for a charity, taking courses at college, running after job interviews and helping mothers in difficulty. I also started a family. But all of this wasn't enough for all the Brexiteers who surround me. How painful it was to read their victory posts on social media even though they destroyed my family, my child's future. Displaying their intolerance was more important to them than showing any sign of compassion. I have no friends anymore. They are insensitive to the xenophobic attacks my baby and I have suffered. They pretend all is ok. I'm not going to try to apply for PR or any other paperwork, as I know I won't qualify. I hope to move back to France before the end of 2019. My partner insists on the wait and see method but whatever is the outcome, I'm not gonna feel at home here anymore. I have been wounded too deeply.

Sophie Ferrand, France

★★★

After gaining my Nursing Diploma in I undertook a degree in Management of the Critical Care Patient and then worked in various very busy A&E's around Barcelona. Work was intermittent, so I decided to pursue my career in England. I came to the UK 17 years ago to pursue my dream of becoming a nurse. I landed in Luton on bonfire night with just £50 in my pocket and a suitcase full of hope.

Unfortunately, my English was not good enough to be working in A&E, primarily because, in my opinion, they speak another language in Yorkshire! I therefore worked in the intensive therapy unit, where the ventilators, pumps and gadgets played to my interests. However, my primary focus was technology; I became very 'Competent' but Care, Compassion, Communication, Courage and Commitment were not my priority.

All that changed one weekend when I was allocated to take care of a young lad who had been in a car accident. He was being nursed in a cubicle; his body was battered red, with multiple fractures. At the time, he was the ideal patient for me as my nurse vision was primarily performing tasks. But towards the end of the shift he asked me what was outside the little window at the end of the cubicle. The following day he again asked me what I could see from the window, and if I could move his bed close to it. Initially I thought he was joking, but he was dead serious. I told him it would be physically impossible.

That night I went home and I couldn't stop thinking about his request. I asked him if he wanted to see the view. I still remember his face; it lit up with a big smile from ear to ear. It took me nearly two hours to manoeuvre all the equipment safely around the room, but I was determined! We finally made it, and like a miracle, a ray of sunshine came through the window and illuminated his face. He asked me to sit on his bed next to him, and for the next half an hour we were sat in silence holding hands. It was a powerful moment and we both ended up with tears rolling down our cheeks. For the first time I understood what Care and Compassion meant. On that day I fell in love with nursing; my job became my passion. I still remember that immense feeling inside me that on that day – I made a difference to somebody. For the first time I was proud of being a nurse.

But now all my career and hard work has been threatening by uncertainty. Since Brexit my life is on hold and my future and the future of my family is unknown. I love England and I have raised my family here. My kids are British. I have never had any problem or felt discriminated against, but since Brexit, I've started to feel like a second class citizen just because of my accent. I have been attacked on social media and what makes me even angrier is that my kids are being affected.

A year ago my 14 years old son asked me if I was going to be forced to go back to Spain if Brexit goes ahead and a year on I still have no answer. My daughter, aged 11, came home crying from school the other day and when I asked her why she told me that another child told her that I was not welcome in the UK and that I would be thrown out very soon. My daughter was heartbroken and asked me if that was true. I could not in all honesty say no! Is it right that my daughter doesn't want to go on holidays to Spain this year to see her grandparents because she fears I will not be able to come back?

Many of us are left feeling unwelcome and uncertain about whether we and our families will have the right to live and work in the UK after Brexit. The refusal of the Westminster government to guarantee our right to continue contributing to our health service is causing a significant number of us to consider leaving the UK, regardless of what future agreement is reached. For how long must our lives and futures be on hold? The current situation is unacceptable. We are people with feelings not 'negotiating capital'. The UK is our home and the government must guarantee the rights of EU nationals in the UK immediately and not, as has been hinted, at some distant point in the future.

Vague assurances are not enough. Our lives have been put in limbo since Brexit. We are facing an uncertain and bleak future in the wake of the referendum result and the anguish and on-going stress that this is causing to individuals and families is immense.

We came to the UK in good faith and we have made our home and our lives here. We contribute on every level and in every sector of British society. Many EU nationals are already severely affected by the current Home Office stance and families are being torn apart.

Seventeen years ago, I was warmly invited to build my life here. I was told it was my home from home. I was told I could settle down, marry a Brit and make my life here. Yet today I am told I'm a foreigner and should go back where I come from. Things are getting so bad that many of my fellow EU citizens hardly dare to speak their own language on the streets for fear of being insulted or attacked. Our very own identity is being challenged, our future, our life. Diversity is what makes a society prosper. I was born in Spain but lived most of my adulthood life in Britain. I am British! Diversity is what made Britain so special, what has made Britain great: its soft power, a mixture of charm, tolerance, creative spirit and openness. Immigrants are not the problem, xenophobia is. We need to stop this madness.

Joan Pons Laplana, Spain

★★★

I am a 71-year-old Italian lady that has lived in this country for a very long time.

When in June of last year Brexit came about, I was shocked, saddened and disappointed but somehow hoped that something may change. Considering that it was all based on a lie, I hoped that common sense would prevail, alas no.

All my friends and acquaintances are people of my age or older, so I know that the mentality of some of them is still nostalgic of their imperialist past. It was impossible to make them understand my disappointment.

True I don't have to worry about jobs now that I am retired. I don't have to go through the great difficulty that young people have with the uncertainty of staying or leaving.

However, I feel I am surrounded by selfish, narrow-minded people with no interest in trying to understand what all this really means; on the contrary, they rejoice in thinking that they have got their country back. Maybe they are hoping to go back to the colonies.

I will have to learn to live with it but it is not going to be easy. It leaves me lonely and isolated, especially now that my husband is no longer with me. Back in Italy, I have no one left.

S. Parsons, Italy

★★★

Picture the scene.

I, an EU national, a proud European with German nationality, went for dinner the other day with one Leave voter and one Remain voter, both British.

"How are you doing?" they asked.
"Yeah – lots on, studying on the side, and Brexit shite, the usual."
"Brexit shite? What's that?"
"Well... do you really wanna go there? Ok then..."

From here I launched into a ten-minute monologue – calm, collected, yet passionate, citing facts and realities – about the plight of the non-British

EU nationals at this time in the UK. Their two faces got longer: Leave-y growing a sort of suspicious frowning, Remain-y just plain surprised. Both listening at me intently. I talked about the PR application I am currently working on.

"So," they wondered, "what's required, apart from the obvious documents?"
"What are 'the obvious documents' in your view?" I asked.
"Well, birth certificate...?"

So, I talked about the four kilos of paper I had been gathering between July 2016 and now, in order to provide 'evidence' of exercising my treaty rights for five continuous years, in the hope it's enough to obtain the approval for the card.

"Four kilos?" Followed by an incredulous "Noooo, whatttt, reeeeally???"
"Yes, four kilos. And yes, it's insane. And no, I'm not making it up. And I'm even a fairly straightforward case."

I talked about how unsettling it all is. I talked about the cases of people being rejected for minor issues with their applications or evidence documents, cases which were published in the media. I talked about, the fact it does not make a difference if you're married to a British person and that 'people like me' do not have it easier.

"Ah come oooooon," Leave-y interjected, "I am 100% sure, people with your skills, people with your professional experience, 'people like you', will NOT be rejected. You won't have any issues, Steffi. This is NOT what people voting Leave wanted; we did NOT mean people like you. All will be fine."

"All will be fine? All will be F*CKING FINE? What about solidarity? What about the stories of fellow Germans getting dog shit through their letterbox? What about the British-born guy, with German parents, who was asked to do the UK citizenship tests despite being born and raised in the UK? What about stories from other non-British EU nationals being rejected for PR for stupid non-reasons? All will be fine?"

"Well, that's just bureaucracy. It's the EU doing this."

"W.H.A.T.? This is happening here. In the UK. The UK government has a choice."

"Well, no, it's bureaucracy dictated by the EU", says Leave-y.

(And BREATHE.) "Ok," I said, "it's not true, but never mind... In any case, ALL Theresa May needs to do is make ONE statement, guaranteeing our rights now and there, to end this uncertainty for us. We came here in good faith under EU law; we settled and made a life not thinking this would ever have to end, or that we will have to make life-changing decisions out of nowhere. My British friends in Germany seem to be treated miles better, they don't have to send away their original passports or national ID cards for months like we do; they don't get extra hurdles thrown in the way, which we need immigration lawyers to unpick for us in order to understand the pitfalls. My fellow EU citizens abroad seem to be able to gain citizenship in no time, and even accompanied by a friendly smile of an actual person who sorts things for them there and then. The UK has a CHOICE."

"Ah well," Leave-y said, "that's classic negotiation. You don't give something, before you have established what you might be receiving back."

"Right...well," I said, "I'm sorry but I am not a bargaining chip. My accrued pension rights are not there to be used in a DEAL, so that the UK can choose and cherry-pick. Are you saying this is ok?"

Leave-y went on launching into analogies: "Well, it's not right to be part of a club where you sit in their restaurant, and they are saying: 'if you want THIS from the menu, you can't have THAT though, you have to stick to our rules'. That's not right. It's a flawed system with the EU... People voiced their protest and frustration about that with the Referendum."

"Right," I said. "So what about the peace project EU, after all it started after the war, didn't it?"

"After what?"

"The WAR."

"Ah. Yeah."

"Well," I went on, "there's the solidarity initiative called 'One Day without Us' this Monday, which I would like to participate in, in some shape or form."

"Oh interesting, what is the aim of that day?" Remain-y asked

"See, in this restaurant here…we have not been served by a single obviously British person so far – the entire team has Eastern European accents." I explained.

They both sank into their chairs, because: "Oooooooh, don't say something like that out too loud!"

"We've been served in the first place and it was in such a friendly way," I said. "These people are here, they are real. This is REAL. Imagine this place without them. This will be the case next Monday: no EU nationals in the UK working, at all, for a full day."

"Well no that's rubbish," Leave-y insisted. "It's not about that… We didn't MEAN people like that, we didn't mean you… I am GENUINELY sorry that you are having to go through this, but this was about unelected bureaucrats in Brussels."

"They're not unelected."

"They are!"

"No they're not."

I dipped into my last bits of strength: "You see, the Referendum had three major flaws to me – an issue of that complexity should have NEVER been brought before the common people to vote on; fine if you want to GAUGE things as government, but then emphasise it is an advisory measure; and if you must, say it could be considered for implementation with a decent, clear, and documented threshold in place. All that didn't happen."

Remain-y looked at me: "I fully agree with every single point you made there."

Leave-y paused.

And then said: "The Referendum was not advisory."

"It was. I can show you the official page where it's written, and the relevant bits highlighted."

"No it wasn't."

"Anyway," I then said, "there's a pro-European March in London, on 25th March, where I will proudly walk with a blue face and yellow stars."

Leave-y is confused: "Really? But... but... what are you marching for?"

"EUROPE!"

"But we like Europe! It doesn't make sense to march for that, that's pointless! And we didn't mean YOU! It will all be FINE!"

P.S. This scene really happened... I left out a lot of detail and focused on the most frustrating elements. And my final paperwork actually weighed 5kg.

Steffi, Germany

★★★

Britain, the tolerant and open country I have loved passionately ever since I arrived here in 1984 as one of the very first Erasmus exchange students (we were pioneers!), has changed beyond recognition within the space of a few months.

Thirty odd years ago, I was warmly invited to build my life here. I was told it was my home from home. I was told I could settle down, marry a Brit and make my life here. Today my English husband and I have been married for twenty seven years. I've never felt like a migrant; I was a European at home in Europe. Yet now neither my three decades spent here, nor my marriage, nor the PhD in English Literature I so enjoyed studying for and passing in a British university, nor the PGCE that made me a qualified teacher, none of these things matter anymore. I cannot even be sure I will be allowed to stay here after Brexit. I cannot get a PR Card because my life has been non-linear and I had never heard of the CSI 'self-sufficient' people like me are supposed to have had since 2006 (an insurance whose legality the EU has been challenging since 2012).

I am told by the government I may not belong here anymore after Brexit, and I am called a bloody foreigner who should go back where she comes from by xenophobes empowered by your anti-immigration stance. Hate crimes against EU citizens here have gone up by 40% since the Referendum. Things have got so bad that many of my fellow EU citizens hardly dare to speak their own language on the streets for fear of being insulted or attacked. Our very own identity is being challenged, our future, our life.

Dr V. Martin, France

★★★

My mum paid a visit last December. Because of the xenophobic times we are living in, I strongly suggested her not to speak in Spanish in public for security reasons. Also to avoid conflicts, as much as possible. However, in a supermarket she was mistreated by a cashier and the manager who refused to take her Spanish ID as evidence of her identity. They confused her nationality by the way. The main thing is that they refused to accept a foreign ID card. She described the situation as being badly shouted at. Even though they had already swiped her credit card, the transaction was declined.

She came back in shock. Some people say that it is an objective policy of the supermarket, but I am sure that shouting at customers and mistreatment is not part of that policy.

M., Spain

★★★

I originally came to Scotland for four months in 2000 as work experience while in catering school in France (I chose Scotland as it was my dream). This is when I totally fell in love with the place, the culture and most importantly the people. I went back to France but I felt like a fish out of water. The hotel where I worked needed staff for Xmas and New Year and paid for my travel to work there for three weeks as they were short staffed. I did go back to catering school afterwards but after a week I was home sick: I needed to get back to Scotland. Since the hotel was really short staffed they offered me a live-in position.

As I wanted to be more in the Highlands I found a live-in position on the Isle of Skye. I finally found the place where I would spend the rest of life. After five years I moved to Glasgow to be able to work and take an English Higher so I could have a more secure job back on the island. I passed it and moved back finding a job with a bank. Unfortunately, in 2011 I ended up in a wheelchair due to muscular dystrophy (I am lucky it is not degenerative and I am really independent). Living on Skye was sadly no longer an option anymore as nothing was adapted. My parents wanted me to go back to France but after all the previous hard time I had overcome I wasn't going to have a wheelchair forcing me to leave the country I call home.

I moved down to Edinburgh (originally with a job lined up but it fell through at the last minute). Nonetheless, I passed a Higher in Psychology, wanted to go back to study but couldn't afford it, so I found a part time job (I can't work full time). Three years ago I met the man of my dreams, a true Scot and I will marry him in just over four weeks.

The past few months have been really hard on us. A side of me doesn't want to put a burden on him with the uncertain future ahead, but apparently I don't have a choice, as he will follow me wherever we need to go, even Timbuktu I am sad, and raging at the same time. These are supposed to be the happiest days of my life preparing for my wedding and instead I cry every time I see bad news regarding EU citizens and Brexit. I worry, I hardly sleep, and I have become really bitter. I haven't applied for PR yet as I'm struggling to find paperwork dating from 12 years ago (when I was working full time and not disabled). I don't want to leave. My all working life has been in Scotland. I did everything to stay here (even horrible jobs like packing prawns at 1am and cleaning pub toilets !). And now the wheelchair will probably be my downfall as I had no CSI when I was unemployed, when I first move to Edinburgh. I want this nightmare to stop. I want to get up again on June 22nd when the only thing worrying me was the fact that I still didn't find a dress suitable for the wheelchair.

Gwendoline MacDonald, France

★★★

On June the 23rd I went to sleep as normal. I have since pretty much forgotten what normal feels like.

I fell in love with London on my very first visit as a young teen. I came here with my family, and I had never felt at home anywhere as I did here. Right there and then I made the decision that one day, this city would be my home. And years later, in 1993, I arrived in London with my suitcase, I had a place lined up at an English course (not because I needed to learn English, but because my parents wouldn't have let me go otherwise), and a shared room with a Japanese girl in a student house in West Hampstead.

I had the time of my life exploring this wonderful, bustling multicultural city. I did the usual Scandi thing of working as an Au Pair, I went clubbing at The Astoria, The Wag and The Hellfire Club. I saw new bands play at The Marquee whenever I had the chance to. And I met the father of my child who is now in her teens. We split up after just over a decade, but there was never one moment where I thought that I should head back to Sweden, because although I was always fiercely proud of my roots, London was now my home.

I set up my own business, I met the love of my life, my teen thrives at school and has a great life here. All was very rosy. Then suddenly there was this Referendum... and on June 24th I woke up in the middle of a nightmare, just like the other three million EU citizens living in the UK, just like the Brits living abroad in other EU countries, just like the 48% who had voted Remain.

My life here had never been under threat. But now there were suddenly no guarantees that I or the millions of other EU citizens living in the UK could remain here. Suddenly we found ourselves being referred to as bargaining chips. Suddenly our futures in this country were uncertain, completely out of our hands, and in the hands of people who seemingly just don't want us here.

Groups like 'Worrying Signs' formed, with people reporting daily acts of hatred against EU citizens by people who think that we are vermin who should 'Go Home'... but this IS our home. Tabloid rags such as *The Daily Mail, The Sun* and *The Express* had been inciting hatred against citizens for months and months leading up to the EU Referendum. The far right organisations joined the coat tails of the Leave campaign, and saw the win as a green card to tell us all, "Leave!"

The day after the Referendum, I started a support group on Facebook for 'EU Citizens in the UK and Brits living abroad', and we have grown in numbers since. We share the same worries and fear. Will we be able to remain in our adopted countries? Will we get to stay? If we get to stay, under what conditions will it be?

We never had a reason to apply for permanent residence prior to the Referendum, but now we all share the same headache over filling out the most intrusive forms which we hope will enable us to stay in this country, in our homes. But not everyone will get their applications for PR approved. Women married to Brits who have stayed at home raising their children, they don't qualify. Students don't always qualify. The majority of us have lived here for years, we have been paying our taxes and national insurance, we contribute financially to British society. Why should we be punished for asking to retain the rights that we now have, the same rights as everyone else living in this country? And if your application for PR gets declined, then you cannot apply for naturalisation. And where do people in that situation stand once Britain officially leaves the EU?

Many worried children can't be reassured that their mothers and fathers will be able to remain here, that everything will carry on as before; that they will be allowed to remain in the country where most of them were born and raised; that they will be able to remain in their schools with their friends. How do you think they feel? This is not their fault. How do you think we, their parents, feel?

Many of us no longer feel wanted in the country that we made our home. Many of us feel afraid to speak in our native tongue in public, just in case someone will tell us to "Go Home!" People try to switch off from their worries, but how can they? How can they sleep peacefully at night when they don't know what the future has in store for them? Sure, no one knows what's around the corner. But the UK is our home. This is where we have put down our roots. This is where our families, our jobs, our friends and our lives are. And to be told that we are safe "for now" but that no one knows what will happen once Article 50 has been triggered and those two years of negotiations are up? That is mental abuse, is it not? We are human beings. We are not bargaining chips. We are not numbers. We are part of the British society, and without us here, without our contributions, where would this country be?

Kristina Strömberg, Sweden

★★★

I wish Brexit didn't happen…

I'm from Poland originally and I've been living in England for over 11 years now. I came to this country to study and it has been the most amazing time. I considered England as my home until the post Brexit events/talks that has shaken me a little. I don't have any family here, they all back in Poland. I've met my partner, who is British, nearly seven years ago and we are expecting our first baby this June, which is really exciting. I've never claimed any benefits, never was late with any payments, been paying all the taxes and never had any problems with the police etc. I've been working really hard for the last ten years and three years ago I've opened my own business, which supports the British industry. This country has been my life!

I'm stressed about UK leaving the EU as I don't know what happen with my future and most of all my child's future. I'm at this stage now that if it wasn't for my partner and the baby I would go back home, there is no question about that.

I've decided not to apply for PR as I simply don't have time to deal with all the pages documents and paperwork. I'm a European and we are in Europe, I do have rights to live here. I've contributed to British economy a lot and it will be their loss if they want to 'send me back'.

Someone shouted at me, "Go back home!" the other day (to a pregnant girl!) but I won't let the minority belittle or frighten me. I'm a human being, I'm a European and I'm strong no matter what.

I wish Brexit didn't happen…

Agnieszka, Poland

★★★

I came here over 22 years ago as an EU student. The Greek government paid my tuition fees, whilst my parents paid for my living expenses. I got a Bachelor's degree with First Class Honours and have worked continuously without a break in employment since I graduated 19 years ago.

I met my English husband only three months after I arrived. We had a long distance relationship at first as he was studying in a different city. After I finished my degree, I decided to stay on because I had fallen in love with life here and, of course, because the love of my life lived here. I got a job easily and haven't had any problem keeping a job or changing jobs when I needed a new challenge. I have never had a high paying job but I earn enough to pay the bills and enjoy life.

Life has been kind to me. I had a very happy childhood growing up in the USA and Greece and then I came to live here in England, where I have lived all my adult life. I have always been made to feel welcome here. My husband and I made many lifelong friends at uni who we still see, and I also have many lifelong school friends who live all over the globe. We had a great time in our 20s, working, earning our modest living and enjoying our social life. After ten years of dating we finally had our big fat Greek wedding and, as is typical of my generation, promptly bought our house and started our family. I feel blessed to have two beautiful children, a loving supportive extended family abroad and the love and support of my English in-laws who live a couple of hours away.

On a personal level, things have been pretty difficult the last seven years because, first, my eldest son was diagnosed with a severe learning and behavioural disability, and a year later my husband contracted a chronic illness. After battling with this illness for years, he is now facing medical retirement at the young age of only 40 years old. I am working full time and am also a carer for my husband and our eldest son, both of whom are registered disabled, as well as looking after our younger son. I am exhausted! And often at the end of my tether.

Last year my husband had a nervous breakdown. It's a very slow process but he is slowly recovering in terms of his mental health. However, he is still struggling with severe anxiety and agoraphobia as well as depression. About a month after his breakdown, Brexit happened. Or rather, that Ridiculous Referendum, which after over 20 years here I had no right to vote in. My British husband did vote (to remain) and when he woke up the next day he was furious at the result and took it very badly, which is understandable. It was me reassuring him that everything would be OK.

I don't really plan to apply for British citizenship but I now plan to apply for PR. I have gotten as far as printing the forms off. My life is full of juggling work with medical appointments for my son and husband and filling in forms to get them the right support. Recently my own mental health has been bad as it's all getting on top of me. I know the PR forms are important but I can barely keep up with everything else at the moment. Add to that the expected triggering of Article 50 next week on, as my husband puts it, my 'Brexit Birthday' (because, yes, the final insult is that the triggering of Article 50 falls on my actual birthday) and I am feeling slightly anxious I've left it too late to apply for PR (will the fees go up? Will the rules change?). Did I mention I've faced redundancy three times in the past year as well? I beg everyone's forgiveness but I am slightly cranky these days!

Anyway, back to Brexit. Most of my colleagues voted to leave. My in-laws probably voted to leave. But I also know you can still love someone even if you are at odds politically. So I take none of this personally. That said, it's been a disappointing year. To say the least.

Regards options, post-Brexit: my own family will NEVER leave the UK even in our wildest dreams. I think there's something comforting about the lack of options you have when there are disabled people in the family. No dilemmas. There is nowhere better we can be than in the UK because of our circumstances. The NHS, DLA, PIP, tax credits. This is a society that supports its citizens and treats people with dignity and respect. I have mostly worked in the public sector and NEVER had any problems about anyone claiming benefits or thought I was any better than anyone else. I am aware I have been privileged with a better education and more options than some, but I truly believe most people are inherently good and do the best they can with the options they have and the 'hand' they've been dealt. Imagine my surprise when my charmed life turned upside down and I had to start applying for practical and financial support! You couldn't make these things up, sometimes.

I may be time-poor and frazzled but I have no financial worries. My British son and husband have good free medical care and also receive disability benefits. Both of my sons get a good free education, the eldest one's education being highly specialised due to his condition. We get regular respite care for him. I am working so still earning my keep and paying my taxes, NI, pension. I am going to live here FOREVER AND EVER, whilst sticking two fingers up at anyone who has a problem with that.

MY home, MY family, MY community, MY country. There are racist, xenophobic, nationalist people all over the world. You can't run away from that. You can stay and fight and make a difference by countering the small-mindedness with your own world view.

Brexit has been upsetting but it will not change my life if I don't let it. I'm a fighter (and I'm pretty mad at the moment) and I will stay. My family are my priority, they are British, I am not. For me, it's a no-brainer.

I am actually willing for loads of things to go tits-up in the aftermath of Brexit, even if it affects our family's standard of living. The value of sterling to plummet, Brexiters' own plans to retire in the sun made impossible, no one to fill all the service, technical, skilled and unskilled jobs that all my fellow EU citizens do so wonderfully. Why? So I can muster up all my indignity and with my typical Greek forthrightness say to all those that voted Leave: "Καλά να πάθετε!" You got what you deserve. It will feel good for all of ten minutes.

M.K., Greece

★★★

For me one of the worst things is the psychological impact Brexit is having. Having been told in the supermarket to "go back home" I started paying only at the self-service check outs. Now I have become proud again of my accent. I guess it was a bit like a bereavement at first and I am moving on and I don't care if Brexiteers like it or not. However, the anger inside me remains. I don't understand how my own in-laws could have voted for Brexit. I hate it when people tell me, "You are different – you will be ok," as if there is some sort of class system of European migrants in the UK.

I find myself having to reassure my youngest child at night that things will be ok. I feel cheated that the country I made my home made me a bargaining chip and made my family feel insecure.

I have only ever paid taxes in the UK. In fact, I have never been an adult in Germany so would not know where to start, should I have to go back, with everything, including housing, taxes, healthcare...

We are now selling our home to set up home in Portugal. I know as much about living in Portugal as I do about living in Germany so we figured we might as well start new all over. If at all possible we would like to stay until our youngest finishes school in four years' time but this may not be possible. Even then we don't know if my husband is allowed to live and work in Portugal.

For my own sanity I have to find positives: I have found out that my husband would go to the end of the earth with me. When we leave we will leave together and with a joint dream of a future. We are both learning to speak Portuguese and I found out how easy it is to learn another language when you speak more than just English. And really importantly, I have made new friends who share my experience of Brexit and who understand my anger, hurt and disbelief. I have also started to feel blessed that I have another 27 countries to choose to live in.

Iana, Germany

★★★

I came to England from Lithuania when I was 16 for a summer holiday and made a rash decision to stay. Since then I attended college, then university and have now been in full time employment for the past three years. I am 25 now and intend to study further, however have put these plans on hold until my husband and I have decided which country we will settle in.

I was invited to my friend's (British) 40th birthday party at Wetherspoons. I was never a great fan of Spoons anyway, however since the Referendum I've refused to attend it on any occasion as it was a very pro-leave pub and I felt I'd rather support other businesses. I did think it would have been considered rude of me to miss his birthday party due to a purely political reason, especially since he had recently attended my wedding. I got my husband, his brother and father (all British) to come along for company as I did not know anyone else who had been invited, except for the birthday boy.

The evening was fine, until my friend asked me if I got my passport yet. I wasn't on the ball and assumed he was referring to all the paperwork associated with surname change after marriage. I told him I had changed my surname at work, with banks etc but because my passport doesn't expire for another three years I was in no rush to have it changed yet. I said I was planning to go back to Lithuania on a holiday once our child is born and get all documents sorted then. My friend then proceeded to tell me I should get my passport sooner rather than later since the Article 50 had now been triggered and how lucky I was having married a Brit.

This is when the penny dropped. I could see my father in law downing his pint in a hurry, anticipating our imminent departure (brownie points to him). I told my friend I had no intention of getting a British passport in the first place as I consider myself EU citizen, to which he replied – "yeah yeah, the passport was the whole reason of you getting married." It was at that point I gave 'the look' to my husband, who was sat across the table from us and none the wiser as to the conversation I was having, however swiftly encouraged his brother to drink up. I didn't want to get into an argument or some political debate and therefore just repeated what I had said before and told him that I have no fear of leaving this country if it ever came to it. His response was yet another "yeah yeah," at which point I told him we had to go. My blood was boiling though. Not only because he reduced my long term relationship and subsequent marriage to a calculated attempt to gain citizenship (which is a misinformed view in any case), but also the smugness in his outlook of British nationality being somewhat better or worth more than mine. I was also angry at how the current uncertainty many Europeans face at this time is unacknowledged by people like the one I considered to be a friend of mine.

My father in law told his wife of the incident and she texted me first thing in the morning saying: "with friends like that – who needs enemies." This, however, came as a surprise to me as both my in-laws were leave voters, who have, after endless discussions, now opened their eyes (even if a little) to the true impact of this country's vote to which they contributed. They're even talking of moving to Spain now (oh the irony).

E.M.C., Lithuania

★★★

I grew up in the Communist bloc. I remember the lack of pretty much everything in the shops, the electricity going off for hours every evening and the hot water bottles my mum used to place under my feet when I was doing my homework (sometimes by candle light) because the radiators were freezing cold in the middle of the winter. I remember all these fondly, because my parents always found a way to make things fun (like cuddling up together under the duvet during dark and cold evenings in winter to stay warm whilst playing word games to pass the time) and protect me from what I now understand – as a parent myself – was a very difficult time for them.

I remember less fondly the lack of freedom to speak up or travel outside of the Communist bloc and the controlled media, especially the national TV, where all you could watch was one hour of praise to our 'glorious leader' followed by a film about workers happily toiling away on a muddy construction site to make the country great. My worse memories, however, are of the checks that my father – a sailor who had access to the 'developed world' due to his job – had to endure from the security services every year and the constant fear that an over-zealous neighbour could file a report filled with lies that could cause him to lose his job or worse. I lived through the 1989 revolution which – for the 13 year old me – was both exciting and terrifying: I could sense better things coming, but I was scared of the gun fire I could hear outside and feared for my father's safety when he was forcefully 'called to arms' to defend the city against 'terrorists'. Some of these memories are now being brought back by our government's authoritarian approach to Brexit and inhumane behaviour towards people who are not born on these shores.

But, like the rest of you, I too have overcome everything and came out a stronger, better person. I completed my under- and postgraduate education in my country, and I brought the skills I learned with me to the UK, where I created my own job rather than 'steal' anyone else's. My British husband is completely in love with my country and, ironically, after living in Romania for six years, we chose to come to the UK only to give our daughter the chance of a Western education. I say ironically because, after a few years of battling the failings of the school system here, we ended up home-schooling our daughter. This country couldn't even provide us with a good school... But that is fine, because this has made us a very strong family unit and we feel we can battle anything. Our 14-year old daughter has grown up to be very mature for her age and, more importantly, has learned to think for herself and be free. She is learning great lessons from what is going on in the world at the moment and is already thinking about how the future of mankind should be shaped and what her role in that could be.

So, at this time of uncertainty, after overcoming the initial worry and anger, we are now very excited for the future. We might continue to stay here, but we might not. This country's got a last chance to put things right, and we're fighting for it alongside all of you. But time is ticking, and we will not wait forever. There are other places out there, on our beautiful continent. We know that my country would welcome us back with open arms. It might not be as 'developed', it might not have as many motorways or home-delivered groceries, it might be a bit more bureaucratic but it is beautiful, non-judgemental and welcoming. The weather and the people are warm and we have a huge family support network that we can rely on. And, for those who count material things above everything else, yes, we could have a better standard of living there: our money would go a lot further (which translates into fewer working hours and more family holidays), we would have more friends and human interaction and we would be able to eat better food that is either grown organically in my aunt's village or protected by EU standards and regulations, rather than shipped across the ocean from Trump's America as a result of a 'wonderful' trade deal.

Our final resolution: We will remain strong and positive. We will not accept what's happening and carry on fighting. We will continue to support those at the forefront of this fight. But we are also assessing our other options… And that's because the one thing we will not accept is to contribute to a society where some people are more equal than others and families cannot be certain of their future together.

Diana Wright, Romania

★★★

I am British born and bred married to the most beautiful woman who has been judged because of her country of birth.

Whatever happens I am done with this country and its foul agendas and politics of race and power and poison. I'm applying for a passport and as soon as I have it this United Kingdom, which Brexit will destroy, will not be worth staying in anyway and so I'm leaving with my family, that is my wife, because wherever she is that is my home.

This country has lied to me, broken and destroyed me many times so I ask myself a question why should I remain, why should I keep putting myself and my family through the same?

I am not a man of words, I don't pretend to be, but I know what I feel and I feel that my wife is hated and that I am despised for being too sick to work.

People who come to this country try to make a life for themselves but are lambasted for any reason that can be thought of to make them feel unwelcome, to constantly remind them they're not one of us even if they have lived here for the majority of their life. What this says to me is that the people who do this are seriously and psychologically damaged and they are not getting any better.

Then I stop and think: it is horrific, yes it's hell not knowing what will happen to us but it could be even worse. We could have children or one of us could be sick with a terminal disease. The thought of having those children deported leaving you helpless and only able to watch them slip away! Brexit is a symptom of years, decades of brainwashing tabloid/news media hate for anything wonderful.

Peter, UK

★★★

I do hope it will all be OK in the end and me and my family can live in peace here where we have our home. In the country where my three kids were born. Kids who speak English as first language (they speak Polish same level but somehow chose English as a primary). I do not hold PhDs, nothing special, just average. These are some things I would like to say.

To British people reading this: I do not want to offend you. Some things are targeted at 5% racists out of 52% who want to go out of EU and many were lied to. I HATE RACISM and all its faces. In the media, it seems there is no positive information related to Poland and Polish people.

All I see in so called media is just negative. That Polish person did this or that – to spark hatred against Polish people. All the time trying to put us in bad light. Why I bother myself with so called media? It is because it is popular among Brits and creates opinion.

You think there are so many of us: this is obvious problem for you. But we do jobs your people don't want to do. You say we come from eastern Europe: Poland is in central Europe! It is to east of UK – yes. But UK is Western Europe. Actually I do not really care – it is just good to be exact.

Until a year before the Referendum I was considering myself EU citizen. But it started to change. Now I feel like immigrant – declassed citizen. For long time I was planning to get UK citizenship. We are now in the process of getting PR papers. Two times rejected due to payment problems although there was plenty of money in my account. Because I did gain PR status long ago – I should not be removed from here even If I do not have PR paper for it. My status should be automatically acknowledged. *Lex retro non agit.* I am slowly changing my mind in current situation: do I really want to spend £4000 and never be considered a real part of this country? And the test...The test that many Brits would fail.

I came here because I was invited – invited by employer. Invited by UK being part of EU. Invited by UK accepting Poland in EU. I will be extremely disappointed in Brits if UK would kick me out. My life is here. I came as an adult to UK but I have really grown up here being responsible, having family. Sometimes I feel like the country of my home is slowly changing to hell hole only because of the vote. Will leavers take responsibility for destroying so many lives?

My personal discrimination/racism experiences happened mainly at my previous workplace. Just after the vote, a person came to me (one that never speaks to me usually) asking when I am going.

It flashed in my brain that it is racist, but I could not believe it is true so I dismissed this. Another guy started literally avoiding me. Changing his route when he did spot me. Stopped talking to me – no reason. After the vote – another person started throwing things on my desk...

I also noticed changing faces. This is from very first day I came here but become more frequent now – when I speak first time to some Brits. Their face changes and suddenly you can tell that you are not welcome. I call it changing face but it is more like their body language and actions. What did I do to that person? I did come to steal jobs and benefits, rob houses and rape, I must be dumb because my English sounds odd and I don't understand a couple of words.

And again I don't mean to offend in general. If you read this, it means I dared to share it.

H., Poland

★★★

I was so impressed with the forward thinking and open attitude of this country when I arrived 30+ years ago and settled down quite happily when I met my husband (British from Norwich) a year later. We EU nationals deserve better than what is happening since the Referendum; we are human beings and our needs are not met on so many levels.

We still live in the EU and the Home Office has been telling us that there has been no change to the rights and status of EU citizens in the UK and British citizens in the EU, as a result of the Referendum. Therefore it is totally absurd that I, being married to a Brit for decades and the mother of two British children, do not have formally 'the right to reside in the UK'. It is utterly appalling that I am, along with millions, being used as a bargaining chip, STILL nine months on after the Referendum!

It breaks my heart to read so many crushing stories from EU citizens. When someone's life is already torn apart, being a carer or being cared for, why should they, these people, these human beings, be even more tormented by uncertainty, by the fear of deportation and of being split from their loved ones?

I feel compelled to speak out for those who are living in painful situations of hardship made even worse by Brexit. Whether they're being forced to fill up some unbearably complicated and unreasonable forms and are fearful of their status being unlawful. Someone has to speak out for those who can't and who have far too much to deal with from their difficult circumstances.

Like Owen Jones said: 'I worry now that the things I believe in more than ever, face being buried and discredited by a frighteningly right-wing Tory government. If you have beliefs driven by a sense of humanity, then that same sense of humanity should always influence how you behave.'

As usual it is those who are the most disadvantaged that suffer the most.

Laure Ollivier-Minns, France

★★★

This week was pure horror, even when I have mastered the 'keep a smile on your face' to near perfection. Behind me are five days of horror and five days of fake smiling through it. Worst occurrences this week:

– being told that I must be a bloody foreigner at the supermarket for going in through the wrong side of the door! (I just took that way, as I was feeling unwell and I had to hold on to something to prevent myself from falling). I was not well enough to respond!
– being told by a British person (born and raised in the UK by a British father and an Italian Mother) that he thinks the foreigners are working harder than any British person just to be told by the British government that we all can go home after Brexit because a so-called majority of idiots think they know it all. (I was about to start crying at my desk, but I had to stay professional!)
– when I told somebody that I find the Daily Mail offensive, and I find it offensive hearing citations from that rag, the person reading it and using citations from it told me that I have no clue, as it is a very reliable British Tory Newspaper.
– being told on two occasions this week that I should let it go, as Brexit is going to happen and I cannot do anything about it.
– being told that only idiots believe the shit the 'Remoaners' put out, and reading the Guardian and the Independent makes me either of the two and I can choose what one I want to be.
– being told that we EU migrants take jobs up in the UK to earn British

money, as we would be paid less in our own country.
– being told we EU migrants try just to avoid taxes and benefit from the British system.

If I include today's occurrences, I feel like I should lock myself into a dark room and not come out anymore.

I really do love my job, but today was the day I really thought about typing up my resignation letter and just leaving this country for ever. I have three children living in the UK and their future is as uncertain as mine and my husband's and the lives of three million other EU Nationals living and working here. Our lives have not just been turned upside down, but also inside out. I know I have become very sensitive, and I cannot just laugh things off as I used to, but is that a surprise? I try really hard to keep the smile, to fake the smile, to pretend I am ok…. I am not ok! No, I am not happy! My fibromyalgia is worse than it ever was, and I am surviving and functioning on an amount of tablets which are enough to kill all of the last surviving rhinoceroses in one go.

I was never a quitter but always a rebel. I always stood up for the weaker, the poorer, the ones who were treated unfair. I always was known as the fighter who even kept on fighting when the rest of the troops had put the swords down.

Brexit Voters listen! Our beloved UK used to be an open, welcoming, friendly, multicultural country. What is it now? Hate ridden, xenophobic, lie believing… People are shouting at foreigners, some people are even killing foreigners. The UK has closed its door on children, on innocent children from war ridden countries. Are you not ashamed? Are you not ashamed about what your country has become? Well, I am ashamed for you! I am ashamed of what the country I loved so much has become.

Claudia, Germany

Nine months on from the Referendum, I am still struggling with overwhelming sadness and anger on a daily basis. Having never been a particularly political person before, apart from some lively but safe middle-class dinner party conversations, I now don't quite know how not to be political anymore.

Originally from the Netherlands, I have lived in the UK since 1984, apart from a couple of years back in Holland in the early 90s. I've loved it here, and feel more English than anything else. I love the weather, the tea, the South West Coast Path, the people. But now it all feels different. The Referendum made me feel rejected to the core of my identity. I suddenly realised how European and Dutch and British I felt all at the same time. I felt so disappointed by the vote, and could not help taking it personally.

Having experienced some maddening bureaucracy at the Home Office over my PR application, I decided to contact a journalist. That decision has turned my life upside down. As a result of that I have made many new friends, I have been on television, radio, and given interviews to the press. I'm part of a subgroup of the 3 million which was tasked with dealing with EU national media, embassies, governments and EU institutions. I've attended a mass lobby, been to the House of Lords, met Nick Clegg and several peers. I've travelled to Brussels to meet Michel Barnier. I've gone on my first ever march. So many firsts in less than three months from when my story was first published in the Guardian at the end of December.

I need to learn to channel my sadness and anger, and give it a constructive place. Because at the moment it feels overwhelming and all consuming, and I am struggling to do normal things like meeting friends, reading books, listening to music, or talking about anything other than Brexit. I struggle to concentrate at work, I don't sleep properly. I risk missing all the good in my life, and not seeing the joy that there is all around me, and neglecting time with friends and family.

I am very hopeful that EU nationals' rights will be sorted very soon. But I worry that I will never quite be the same person again. I hope that I can regain some balance – it's been a very steep learning curve.

Monique Hawkins, The Netherlands

★★★

One of the hardest, and scariest, things for a parent to hear is their child saying that they don't see any reason to go on. My 17 year-old cannot yet get citizenship despite tracing her British ancestors back over 400 years due to my fortune of being born in South Africa. It wasn't something that we even thought about when we moved here. She has an EU passport thanks to her Finnish father and we never even considered the possibility of Brexit – seriously, who did?

Now, as a straight A student, her dreams and aspirations of going to university in 2018 are on hold while she and her father are used as bargaining chips. A bright and happy student without a care in the world beyond her studies, she now has panic attacks, nightmares and visions of having to leave all her known family. No indication has been given to the status of students and their fees for 2018. Home fees are bad enough for a working-class family with little to spare at the end of the month. International fees would make it impossible.

I'm sure she is not alone in this problem but she sure feels like she is right now. We finally decided that she should see a counsellor. When she explained to the counsellor that she was having panic attacks etc. due to the uncertainty surrounding Brexit and her future the counsellor said, "Oh, it's not that we don't want you, we just don't want so many of you!" How can a professional who is supposed to help people come up with that statement to anyone, let alone a child? Now she feels even more like a second-class citizen.

I would throw my hands up in the air and say I give up. However, we will continue to raise our children to be tolerant of people who are so narrow minded towards them, we will teach them that being English doesn't make you automatically superior, we will remind them that they do matter and that the world is a far bigger place than one tiny island and it is filled with magical people of all different and wonderful races, colours and cultures.

As a mother, my anger at the injustice of how they are treating all EU residents knows no bounds. As a Brit, I am devastatingly ashamed.

Barbara, British mother of a Finnish daughter

★★★

Brexit was a real punch in the face, a real wakeup call. Like I was naively lived in a bubble and all of a sudden it's gone and I can see clearly now. I see the real face of this country. I came here nine years ago, I started from the very bottom, working in a factory as a line packer on nights, we lived in a shared house, like so many others. We were working super long hours (sometimes 22 hours shifts), it was hard work. But we were happy and young and free. We didn't care about the dirty work, because we earned two times more already than back in our own country (and I had a decent job back in Hungary).

Then I found a little better job, I became a toilet cleaner (yes, that counts as better) in an office building, and we moved in a little, two-bedroom flat with my fiancé. It was just the two of us, finally. I knew I'll have an office job one day, I knew I'll earn an awful lot of money, and we will buy a house. We worked seven days a week, 12 hours a day, but we didn't care. We had a dream and we knew how to reach it. With hard work and more work and even more work. We never applied for any benefits, we always just gave and gave to this country. We haven't been unemployed since we moved here, I don't have kids and I don't send any money home. We completely built our life over here.

So after two years of being in the UK, I managed to find an office job, and I've been there ever since. I was so proud of myself! (I still work crazy hours, and I work in a three shifts pattern – early, late and night shift, doing 12 hours almost every day). Then a year later we bought our own house! A new built, four-bedroom, beautiful house with a little garden, in Manchester's suburban area. We were over the moon and couldn't believe that just after three years of being in the UK, we could afford to buy a house like this.

Like I said we worked super hard for all of this. We've been living our happily ever after, planning our future, saving up to learn and travel and to achieve more goals and be more successful. And then on the morning of the Brexit I had a panic attack. What if all this was for nothing? What if all this will be taken away from us? What if all my hard work in the office in the past seven years, all the cleaning I did in the first two years was a waste?

I couldn't believe what was happening. I still can't believe that the control over my own life had been taken away from me. By people who I know and love. All the people who voted 'leave' put me in this position, even though I've never done anything against any of them. I don't deserve this uncertainty in my life.

Like almost all of us, I feel betrayed. And when people tell me that "it wasn't about you," it just makes me angry. Because it is about me. Maybe when they voted 'leave' they didn't know what the consequences are. But I, we, three millions of us, are paying the price for it.

So I decided to just carry on. With a cold heart. I always wanted to become a British citizen, I even wanted to get rid of my Hungarian one, and be proud to be British in my chosen home. But not anymore. Not like this. I won't be, I can't be proud. It's forced on me, because otherwise I'm in an unsafe position. Otherwise I'm just a secondary citizen. Otherwise I'm unwanted and unwelcome. I'll become British but, in my heart, I won't be able to feel I'm one of them ever again.

Anita Hoffmann, Hungary

PART V

"I feel like I've been cheated on."

Let me tell you about my Cuneo moment. After Mrs May's speech about how she thought European leaders were trying to interfere in her election, something snapped in me. Not just anger, but shame to be part of this nation, this culture, this new direction. I needed to get out of Brexit Britain, even if for just a few days.

The Piedmont region of northern Italy seemed a good a spot as any for some clean air. Last Sunday afternoon, I sat at a pavement cafe in this street in the small town of Cuneo, my face to the warm sun, and felt able to breathe again. Yet simultaneously something became crystal clear to me: I realised that I had fallen out of love with my own nation, my own people. It's like realising you've fallen out of love with your partner, or that you suddenly realise that you feel contempt for your parents or siblings. It is no small thing. I report this moment to you, because I suspect that I am not the only one to have experienced this. I'm still getting used to the idea. I feel removed from my compatriots, no longer feel a sense of 'us', more a sense of 'you lot'. Looking back to the Referendum, my feeling is 'You'll get the country you deserve, but it's not mine'. I love England, I love Kent, I love the chalk downs, the hollow lanes, the sleepy villages with their flint towers, the ancient towns, the wonderful coasts....Who knows, perhaps England needs first to walk through fire to be cleansed of its hubris, to realise that we cannot isolate ourselves from our friends, from the family of nations that has brought us peace and prosperity for seventy years.

Adrian Hackford, England (married to a Dutch citizen)

★★★

A fortune-teller told me when I was 20 that I would live most of my life on an island. This was very good news: I imagined long sandy beaches, palm trees, warmth all year round, blue skies. Lovely. Little did I know then that her prediction would come true, but not quite how I had imagined!

I first came to visit England in 1976, the year of the great drought. I was 13, and what I knew of the UK in these pre-internet days was in stereotypes, Asterix, the reputation for Britain to be wet, and green, and humid, and grey. So, the summer of '76 was the first of the surprises which welcomed me. Derbyshire was like a tundra, brown and crisp, the Peak District rivers were barely flowing, and I fell in love with this country there and then. I can honestly say that England was my first love.

Fast forward a few years, and after travelling and working through a few other countries, I decided to go back to university, studying English, what else. As part of my studies, I could apply to go to the UK as an 'assistante', thus immersing myself in the linguistic bath and teaching French to recalcitrant British kids. I chose to go to Scotland. I was only going for one year, after all, and when would another opportunity like this present itself? Well, you know what they say: men make plans and the gods laugh at them. I met the man who would become my husband, and my fate was sealed, I settled here, in the UK.

Fast forward again, for the rest is terribly banal: three kids, various jobs, marriage, moving from Scotland to England in the Thatcher recession years, more jobs, raising our family, the same as millions of people do, living one's life, that's all; now the kids are mostly grown-up, we were starting to think about retirement in a few years. As my health had been steadily deteriorating over the years, we were thinking that maybe we should retire somewhere warmer, the Canaries sound perfect, I speak Spanish, and my oh-so-British husband could still get his UK commodities there, as there are many British expats living there too.

Then the shattering earthquake that was the Referendum: Suddenly, we have no certainties. I am being made to feel like a stranger in a strange land. Me, for whom nationality was just a matter of fact, like the colour of my eyes, a small inconvenience to have to go to the consulate when my passport runs out, I feel there is an arrow constantly pointing at my head, or maybe a sword of Damocles would be more accurate. I do not know what is going to happen, and I oscillate between fearing the worst and chastising myself for being over-dramatic; I cannot believe my country of adoption could be so callous as to reject me, yet every day this is becoming more and more of a possibility.

Oh, the irony: I was so completely integrated that I had no other EU expat friends, never saw the need to seek my 'own' people, I was quite happy to just potter along with the rest of my British gang of friends. For the first time in my life, I am actively seeking other foreigners to become friends with on social media; I haven't spoken as much French since I was teaching it, over 30 years ago! At least, with them, I feel safer, with like-minded people, who understand my fears and worries because they have the same.

Oh, Britain, it is you rejecting us which is forcing us to dis-integrate. Disintegrate. Funny that. Here's a thought: maybe it is the rejection of all these foreign bodies that will cause the United Kingdom to collapse on itself; maybe it is all these little people with funny accents who will turn out to have been the cement which kept it all together.

Marie-Laurence Pace-Dordain, France

★★★

I am a neuroscientist and ten years ago I moved my laboratory from San Francisco to London. I had been offered a great job at University College London, and my wife and kids were kind enough to follow me as we moved across the globe. We were attracted to the UK because we felt it had the best advantages of Europe and of the US combined.

Ten years later, I still love the job, and the kids feel British, but due to Brexit, the country is rapidly losing that appeal. Part of the reason is the incredible frustration that we are encountering in obtaining PR permits.

My family and I have passports from both the US and the EU (I am Italian, and have lived a lot in the US), and suddenly we need to obtain PR.

We want PR for two reasons. First, we don't know what settlement will be agreed in the negotiations with the EU (possibly, no settlement at all), and we don't want to risk a situation where suddenly millions of us need PR to stay in the country, work, etc. Second, we were denied a vote in the Referendum and we want to make sure we can vote in the future, in general elections or further referendums. For that we need to become citizens, which requires first having PR.

However, the Home Office is making the process of getting PR incredibly arduous. In my case, the application was easy (and it was accepted) because I have a simple employment history, but my wife and kids were not as lucky. She was refused PR because for one year out of last five she did not work, and did not have CSI (which we were unaware one needed). The application from our kids was denied because hers was denied. We appealed, but lost the appeal too.

This is a bitter experience. It will probably get resolved by applying one more time, this time hiring an immigration lawyer. But it is disappointing to see the country treat us this way. My kids feel British (they moved here aged four and six), we paid substantial amounts of taxes for ten years, and in fact I have been a net source of income for the UK. I brought in at least £5 million in research grants from the US and the EU.

So, until now we had not discussed possibly leaving the UK but now we have our eyes open, and if an opportunity arises, we may say goodbye. Indeed, it is hard to feel as welcome as we felt when we arrived, and ultimately if we can't vote at the ballot box, we will vote with our feet.

Professor Matteo Carandini, Italy

★★★

I was 19 years old and it was my first time away from my family-home, back in Gothenburg when I moved to the UK in 2007. I had decided to do an undergraduate degree in psychology with child development as specialisation. My plan had been to finish my degree and then move back to Sweden to continue my career and education. However, I met my now fiancé during my first year and as things went on we decided to settle in London. We thought of moving to Sweden, but as my fiancé isn't the most talented when it comes to learning new languages, it was easier to stay here where we both knew the language and had decent job prospects.

After my degree I wanted to work with children. I volunteered for a few months and then got a job working as a support worker for adults with learning disabilities. This involved working shifts, enabling very vulnerable adults to live a fulfilled life doing things most of us take for granted. It also involved supporting with dressing, toileting, and showering/bathing the service users. Not an easy job, and most of us were non-UK citizens. Later I worked in a school as a learning support assistant supporting children with additional and special educational needs. After my two years working in schools, supporting many children, I decided to do a Master's in 'Child Studies' at King's College London. During my degree I volunteered in a refuge for women that had experienced domestic abuse. I ran play groups and after school clubs for the children that lived there with their mothers and learnt more about the impact of domestic violence/abuse and trauma on child development and the mother–child relationship.

Just before I handed my Master's dissertation in I got offered the job to work as a tutor in a special school for children with complex autism and severe learning disabilities. This job was really challenging, with children there displaying many challenging behaviours, both physical and mental. However, it was one of the best jobs I have had. I worked there for just over two years before I got accepted onto the Doctorate in Educational Psychology, at the University of Exeter. I am now in my last year of the three-year doctorate. Throughout the doctorate I have been placed with a local authority where I have carried out the job of an EP in ever increasing capacity. I am currently the link-EP for six primary schools, co-work two large secondary schools and have four early years cases, which I manage on three days a week. The other two days a week I am working on my doctoral thesis, which is due in next week. I have a job lined up as a fully qualified EP, which starts in September.

Throughout my adult life I have worked for the citizens of this country, I have supported people in very vulnerable states and I have supported them to find hope and overcome different barriers to achieving their potential. On the 23rd June last year I felt so rejected, I felt like my efforts for this country had not been valued, that I was just another 'EU migrant, here to take your jobs'.

A few days before the Referendum my soon-to-be mother-in-law shared a completely ridiculous status update from someone else saying that the reason we now have CVs is due to the EU and its bureaucracy, that university fees were due to the EU, that women HAVE to work due to the EU, etc. I explained to her that this was simply not true, and that she could have her opinion of the EU but that she should perhaps look at the facts. Her answer? Well, she said: "Don't be silly! Why are you taking it personally?!" I explained that I did because if the country voted to leave it would affect my life negatively. She laughed at this and said, "Of course we won't send you home, you're lovely." As if that is how it works. This whole discussion upset me and the fact that no one understood, made it worse.

A few days after the Referendum, I was in a café ordering some coffee, a man walks past me and says: "Don't look so sad! The Polish will be gone soon!" Me and the girl behind the counter just looked at each other, bewildered. The man left and the girl whispered to me "I'm Polish..." I did not know what to say to this. The hatred and hostility from total strangers I felt then was something I had never felt before... And I couldn't even imagine what the girl behind the counter felt.

Now I'm in the process of gathering documents for my PR application. However, due to having worked and studied on and off I need to find proof of my CSI, which I had. However, my CSI was from Sweden and as it was closed when I finished my masters I am having difficulties finding proof that it ever existed. My mum has looked through my childhood home and found some documents, which I hope will be enough. But if not, I'm not sure what the future holds. Some days I question whether I should finish my doctorate or not. Whether the job I have lined up will turn around and say, "Sorry, there's too much hassle in proving that you can work here legally and in two yours time you might need a visa…"

Maria Vukoja, Sweden (with a Czech mother and a Croatian father)

★★★

I am French, but there is a lot of Italian blood in my family, a bit of Austrian blood too. I grew up near the Swiss and German borders. I have always felt pretty much European. I studied English at uni and I came to London as a French assistant in September 2002. It took me two months to decide I wanted to stay in this country. I liked the mix of cultures, the tolerance I noticed, the freedom I had.

In my second year, I trained to be a secondary school teacher. After four years in London, I moved to Leicester where I had found a new teaching job. I met a British man and in 2008, we bought a house near Leicester and we got married in France. We then adopted a cat, who responds to both French and English. I used to joke that "Now that I have a house, am married and have adopted a cat, I am stuck in this country." Our two children, a girl born in 2010 and a boy born in 2014, have both nationalities, British and French. We are a European family. Or so I thought…

The weeks leading to the Referendum caused a few arguments with my husband, we couldn't agree during and after political debates on TV. The day after the Referendum, I found out that my husband had voted 'Leave' – "Because I want the best for our children," he said. Without realising that it could mean a life without their mum. He still doesn't understand my worries. "You've been here for 14 years, you've always worked, you'll be ok!" But I am not OK. I feel betrayed by the man I love…

He does not seem to realise that by voting leave, he has jeopardised my life here and our life here as a family. The uncertainty is unbearable. My parents-in-law also voted leave, as did my husband's aunt and uncle. I used to get on really well with them. But the Referendum broke something. I am polite and civil, but that is it. I struggle to hold conversation with them. My relationship with my husband is at a breaking point. If we did not have the children, I would have left as soon as possible after the Referendum. But I am trying to do what is best for my children, for my family… At least one of my children's parents has to!

I recently had an operation, but still went to the March in London, with my cast and my European flag. The following day, at a family gathering, my father-in-law asked me how things were. And for the first time I mentioned PR that I am collecting evidence for, and citizenship, that I cannot afford. He told me that I may not have the money but that he does. And that I only need to ask. He added that he understands it might go against my principles but the offer is there. Yes, it goes against my principles. I don't want to apply for PR as it is not legally required, I don't want to take the British citizenship… It doesn't feel like a choice. Brexit is taking my freedom away and has shattered my dreams.

C.K., France

★★★

I fell in love with Britain when I stayed with a family in Devon for a language exchange, and even though I wouldn't actually move to Britain until 2013, a decade later, every time I landed at Heathrow on a plane I felt like I had arrived home. I moved here first for an exchange year in Leeds, then internship in London where I started my career in market research. Despite having travelled all around Europe, I felt so at home in the UK I couldn't imagine living anywhere else.

My Scottish partner and I lived in London until this January. We've made a choice to move out of the country because we could no longer see a future together in the UK: we were about to buy a home together but with my rights to stay up in the air, we were faced with making a risky choice or waiting for up to two years for the outcome. Adding to our dilemma, we are 36 and 37 so if we want to have a family, we can't wait forever – and also did not feel comfortable starting a family in the UK given the treatment even half-British children are getting at the moment.

Even though most people assume I was behind the move, it was in fact my fiancé who wanted to leave in an attempt to secure his own European rights. He was worried we would be limiting our options of being able to live together should something happen and I wasn't able to live in the UK anymore so he decided he would rather move out of his own country before Article 50 was triggered, just in case that becomes a cut off point for both EU citizens in the UK and UK citizens in the EU.

But the story isn't so simple. Four years ago I co-founded a company in London, and in the past 18 months we have seen a phenomenal amount of success, growing from two to ten people. Even though I now officially live in Amsterdam, I return to London frequently for work – every trip wrenches my heart because I still love London and Britain like a home, and I didn't want to leave. I also worry for my team as the economic consequences of Brexit could potentially have a devastating impact on our industry and as such our business.

195

I felt that I could never apply for British citizenship as I feel thoroughly betrayed by the country. I've spent most of my adult life in the UK and loved it with all my heart. I worked so hard to fit in and be accepted, and now it feels like that was all an illusion – that people like me were never truly welcome in the first place. I've also paid taxes for 13 years and hardly used public services so I feel like I have been a good 'guest', as some people now call us EU citizens in the UK.

For us, the best choice was to leave – on top of everything else, the emotional distress from the uncertainty was becoming unbearable and made it difficult to recover from the burnout I was diagnosed with last year as burnout itself is often caused by high levels of uncertainty in your life. Moving away has been hard, even though Amsterdam is lovely, because neither of us wanted to leave. I've come to realise it feels like heartbreak – like breaking up with someone when you still love them but you know deep down it's not going to work out in the long run.

I wish more people understood that it's not just EU citizens whose rights to a peaceful family life are being trampled on but also their British partners – the uncertainty over my right to stay came in the way of us starting a family and settling down. After we've left things have become even more worrying than they were when we made our decision and we are no longer sure we'll ever return to Britain – unless Scotland gains independence. Most annoyingly, months of public discussion have now left a niggling doubt in my mind that there is something fundamentally wrong about living in a country other than the one you were born in – even though I know it's not true, there is now a trace of shame and guilt about being a Citizen of the World which was never there before.

Elina H., Finland

★★★

The immigration narrative of Brexit is a 'them' and 'us' scenario. Yet there are so many families like mine: I am a UK national married to a French lady, and our daughter was born in Sweden. My wife moved to the UK in 2002 and worked for six years paying UK tax and NI. Yet the irony was that it was hard to register for NI, no one really cared about registering EU nationals when we enquired. In 2008 we moved to Sweden for my work, and we registered in to the Swedish system. We received the same access as a Swede to health care, etc. And I have to say the Swedish system was far superior to the UK system. We had our daughter whilst in Sweden and then moved back to the UK in 2011. We registered back in the UK for the doctors, electoral register, etc.

Now this is where the problem starts. My wife stayed at home till 2013 to look after our daughter and thus was not paying tax for those two years. We have since been told that my wife should have taken CSI for those two years. Yet at no point did anyone inform us of CSI or the need of my wife to exercise her treaty rights. As a consequence when my wife applied for PR earlier this year she was denied because she has not paid tax for five consecutive years. The time, tax and NI contributions before we went to Sweden do not count. Thus my wife is left in limbo, not knowing if she can remain in the UK after Brexit.

The emotional effect on all of us is clear, we feel betrayed by the government and let down by a poorly managed system that was and still is deceptive. More than once I and my wife have been in tears, yet our friends and family do not acknowledge there is a problem. So many say, "Oh I am sure your wife will be fine," but these dismissive platitudes just compound our feelings of betrayal, because no one wants to admit there is a clearly negative effect to our family.

In the media and wider society we feel like the damage to families like ours has been swept under the carpet. The unfairness in the situation is not acknowledged, and one is left wondering who supports you. I look around my work canteen and think 'well 52% of this room voted to put my family under severe stress'. I am left wondering if there is a lack of empathy in British society, have we as a nation lost sight of our compassion?

Dr Richard Blackwell-Whitehead, UK

★★★

Brexit has created insecurity in my life. I came to the UK aged 19 in 1991, married my English husband a year later and we have had three children. I am the only one in our family to hold a French passport and in the 25 years up to June 2016 I have never felt the need to change that. I have worked on and off for 15 years mostly part-time, I am currently a stay-at-home mum caring for our autistic son and due to health issues of my own, which prevent me from getting the CSI requirement I had never heard of until I began looking into the PR process a couple of months ago. CSI is virtually impossible to get if like me you have a chronic pre-existing condition. Technically in the eyes of the Home Office I'm now considered an illegal immigrant.

Brexit has also created division in my life. For the past eight months the stress and anxiety over my status and my rights post-Brexit have taken their toll on me and my family. This has created a rift in our life. we have had arguments with Leave voters friends and family and I have shed tears on a number of occasions due to our stressful situation.

I have been avoiding my Brexiter in-laws for the past few weeks since the last time when at their house they upset me with their views and the things they said about foreigners and their comments about lazy French people.

Anyway today my husband's parents turned up at our house at 2.45 pm and as soon as they were sat down the conversation took two minutes to turn to Brexit and that didn't go very well. They are both of the opinions that 'foreigners take our houses, our jobs and our benefits and the ordinary people have nothing left' and 'we'll be so much better off out of the EU'. I was sat there listening to them fuming with anger and had to bite my tongue to remain polite. All I could muster was 'well I don't agree with you' several times.

Then I tried again getting through to them by explaining the situation with me and the PR, and they were dismissive saying, "you're not going to be kicked out... that's not going to happen," as if not being kicked out is the only thing I should consider about my life in post-Brexit England.

Then of course because I had mentioned to them before the possibility of having to move back to France with the children and my hubby (their son) it's obvious they aren't happy about that and must have spoken about it between themselves because father-in-law said, "Well, what will he do in France?" (Job-wise they meant, because he speaks hardly any French.) To this I replied, "With the way things are going we may not have a choice soon."

I don't know what they expected me to say. Yes, going to France is far from ideal for my husband's job prospects but I'm not the one who voted for us to be in this situation in the first place. Now I have the feeling that if we do end up leaving I'll be blamed for breaking up the family by having gone back to France. I'm so angry right now.

Nationalistic arrogance isn't always straight cut and in your face. Since the Referendum I've not been faced with a glaring act of xenophobia or intolerance directed at my person, by this I mean no one has said to me directly "You French **** go back home!" But my experience of it has been insidious and more subtle. The silence of the majority of my British friends about our situation has been deafening.

Yesterday I posted a comment about what's happening to me on my Facebook profile. All of a sudden the silent ones have come out of the woodwork to defend their positions.

From the replies I have had it would appear for some that xenophobia and/or racism is only unacceptable and worth speaking against when it targets Muslim people... I am making people sick with my posts about my/our situation... People don't have time or energy to protest for EU nationals' rights (yet the same people have plenty of time to protest about Trump)... Not everyone voted for Brexit but we (EU nationals) are just going to have to wait a couple more years in uncertainty... This country cannot take anymore, the three million here are too many, etc.

Their attitude compounds my feelings of betrayal, disappointment and despair at this country. It's not just what the government is doing or what the likes of UKIP supporters are saying, but the unsupportive insensitive comments and silence of people I considered as friends.

Brexit again has left another bad print on me today. I feel alienated as if it is them and me now.

N.C., France

★★★

I had no job, no prospects of getting my life sorted over there and got to the point that I had no choice but to leave. Then four years ago a good friend of mine paid my plane ticket and came with me to help me find a job and place to stay. He made a good life in the UK and managed to go back to Portugal to have a quite comfortable life. He helped me because the UK has always been good to him throughout the years he stayed, and I always believed it was a beacon of tolerance and multiculturalism. So I filled my backpack with the few things I could bring, left family and girlfriend behind (like so many of us) and came to this adventure to try to become a an art teacher. Started in a small room in Banbury, my girlfriend (also a teacher) came after a few months, as soon as I found a better place for us to be. Made coffees for quite a while, my girlfriend sold burgers. We made friends of many different nationalities and of course, made many British friends, all very curious about my culture and my sunny country. I never felt apart or different. With help of great people we found a way to go forward and recently we managed to start teaching. We built a life for us together, and for the first time in 13 years we have a place we call home! We live in a friendly community, and life has been good.

All changed with the Referendum result. I had to go home that morning because I was too disturbed to work. An idiot who used to work with me asked me if I had bought a ticket already to go back to my country. After that I broke a few 'friendships', couldn't trust anyone, I felt betrayed. As if all that inclusion was fake, a lie. Until that morning I felt part of something great, now I feel I am part of a group that is not welcome for no good reason. When I go to work, I see so many children with their lives potentially destroyed by things that don't matter, that mean nothing... I just can't get it through my mind...

My British friends have been great, they make things much more bearable... They can see my distress. I feel paralyzed with fear, I don't know what to do to stay here, what's the next step to take, if it's best to do nothing, there are horrible stories around. I'm not in the worst situation. I don't have kids, I'm here for only four years but these were the only years in my adult life that I was fully happy and built something for me and my partner. I love this country! It's my home! I love it as much as any British person loves the place they call home... As anyone can call home.

We'll see how it goes... I still have faith that things will be well.

Bruno, Portugal

★★★

Twenty years ago I started to work on a research project and on my PhD thesis in my native Austria with several project partners who were located in other European countries. The project was funded by the European Union.

Four years later, after the completion of this project, I moved the UK with my wife and started to work at one of my project partners, a relatively small manufacturer of mainly aircraft parts. Thanks to the EU our move was easy. We did not even feel as foreigners – we were EU citizens like British people, not foreigners. A few years later we got a son, a British and Austrian citizen. Our company grew, my job was and still is interesting. I am now a technical director.

A lot of our customers are in the EU – especially in Germany, but I was not too concerned about the Referendum. When Leave won I was shocked. I had not seen it coming. For the first time in the UK I felt as an immigrant – a rejected immigrant. Many in my company are from Poland and other EU countries and felt similar.

To protect our business we created a factory in Germany, which we completed recently. A part of our manufacturing, investment and business will in future be there. I will remain in the UK (also because of our son's school), but I am involved in this German subsidiary, the first subsidiary abroad for our 70 year-old British company.

W.B., Austria

★★★

I am an Italian national. I met my British husband in Germany where we both used to work and live happily. We got married and decided to move to the UK in 1994 after our son was born. In 1995 I set up my business as a self-employed translator and interpreter and I have been working as such since then.
I have always loved my job, not least because it has given me the opportunity to work and look after my children at the same time. I have always

loved this country, its language, history, literature, etc. and have always been proud of living in the beautiful city of York, where I have always been treated with respect and consideration.

Although I have been travelling all over Europe for my job, I have always felt that the UK was my home and could not contemplate to live anywhere else. That's why the news in the morning of 24th June was a terrible blow. I started looking at the people around me wondering who was really my friend and who instead wanted to send me back home (which home? This is my home!) in a 'banana boat'. Maybe the people around me did not change but unfortunately my view of them did.

To my dismay I have realized that being married to a British citizen for almost twenty-five years, having two wonderful Anglo-Italian children, having lived, worked, paid taxes, contributions and participated actively to the life in the UK won't ensure me the right to remain in this country. I have never felt the need to apply for British citizenship. I was a free European citizen in a free European country. I felt safe. But then a few weeks ago an article about me was published in my local paper. It was at the time of the House of Lords' voting to guarantee our rights. It was a brief article about European citizens living in limbo since the referendum. The reaction to the online version was terrible. Apart from a few encouraging comments, there were lots and lots of insults. I stopped reading after seventy entries… I was supposed to be interviewed by the local BBC channel too, but my children were so distraught that they begged me not to do it. I was (am) not afraid but very disappointed. The majority of York voted to remain but the Brexiters are very vocal. I have decided to apply for the permanent residence card, but I am self-employed and therefore I belong to the category of 'difficult cases'. I am not sure what is going to happen in the future. I sometimes hope to wake up and this is just a bad dream.

Antonella Gramola Sands, Italy

★★★

US AND YOU

We want to be rid of people like you
Just like you, but not you
You can stay
You're furniture
You're post-welcome
Here

We want to be rid of people like you
Just like you, but not you
You can pick my fruits
You can pour my coffee
You can care for
My mum

We want to be rid of people like you
Just like you, but not you
So I will buy us a proper pint
To celebrate our post-friendship
Can't you reach a state of post-hurt?

Saskia Slottje, The Netherlands

★★★

Nobody thought it will last when I arrived in the UK in 1992 to start my life with James. We came from different backgrounds and he was older than me with a muscular wasting disease. But I was in love with him. He spoke five languages perfectly and he had an amazing mind. What is incredible is how he made something of himself with all the odds against him. Youngest of five and the son of a labourer with no money. But he did. He moved to Europe for a while and educated himself. For the first two years he supported me financially until I could find a job. We also went to university together and worked in the same firm.

Then he was rushed to hospital and had to have a tracheotomy tube fit in. This is when I realised his family did not accept me because they found excuses not to help me. They found excuses not to come for dinner. Foreign food I guess. Twenty years living together and hardly any support, just excuses not to come for lunch or dinner, it is too much for you.

Unfortunately, my mother was diagnosed with cancer and for six months I was backwards and forwards home to see her. She passed away after six months and I was back in the UK full time.

Then James got really ill and passed away after a month in hospital and no visitors no support. Couldn't understand why.

Then Brexit came along and suddenly they felt entitled to tell me they didn't like outsiders, I was not one of them, I was just a rich spoilt child. I wasn't thinking clearly then I felt like a puppy you kick several times and come back for more. I tried desperately for them to like me. I loved their brother. I cared for him, so why don't they like me, why?

We couldn't have children. It was too risky but I had twenty wonderful years with a very special human being trapped in the wrong body. I feel blessed. Everyone who met him loved him, he was very special. I am very lucky to have met him. He loved me, looked after me too and taught me a lot about life. I wonder sometimes if he was adopted. Very different to the rest of his family intellectually and as a human being. He was very sensitive and kind.

Sorry if I haven't written clearly enough. Too many emotions. It is too raw. No I am not a bloody foreigner, an outsider. I am a human being who has lost the love of her life. A bit of humanity and understanding won't go amiss. I have not had the mental strength to go down the route of getting PR.

Anonymous, Spain

★★★

I came to the UK in 2014 via the Erasmus Student exchange programme, as I was finishing my (second) master's. From the very beginning I was fascinated by the country, the people, the atmosphere and everything. Everyone here seemed so nice, polite, friendly and welcoming, that I could hardly believe it. It seemed like xenophobia, homophobia, racism, sexism and all sorts of discrimination were totally non-existent. At the end of my stay the University secretary asked me how I liked it here and when I said that I loved it, that the people are nice and friendly, she laughed and said, "Oh really? Where did you find those nice and friendly people?" At the time it seemed like a joke, but just two years later those words turned out prophetic.

After the three months of the Erasmus Programme I came back to my country to finish my studies, but it was not long before I decided to go back to the country I had so deeply fallen in love with. I moved back here in August 2015 on my own, with only a suitcase, a one-way ticket and the strong determination that I could make it. It wasn't easy at first. I couldn't even get a job as a cleaner, because "I hadn't got experience".

For a short while I was a warehouse worker – carrying heavy loads, pushing trolleys, etc and not moaning even for a second. Finally I managed to find a wonderful job as an interpreter, which is actually what I'd studied for. Needless to say, I haven't had a penny out of the British system that hasn't been earned. Meanwhile I met my wonderful British partner whom I love more than anything and we're planning to get married within the next months. He's been to my country with me a couple of times now and he loves it. He knows my family, and I know his, and we all seemed to get on perfectly, but... Ah well, I guess it was just too good to last, as they say.

On the morning after the referendum, I couldn't believe what I heard. I was pretty much ready for the news, but I wasn't happy of course. I knew my partner's parents and most of the family had voted to leave and they weren't even a bit ashamed to discuss it in front of me. Still at that point I thought it would be okay for those of us already here.

Now, almost a year after the referendum, other than general talk about how "they'll think of something" and "it'll be alright", we haven't had any written or legal reassurance whatsoever! There are people who've lived here not for years but for decades and they've got children or even grandchildren who are legally British citizens, yet there's no guarantee even for them (other than those who've got a PR or citizenship, who I'm afraid are a very small percentage)! If someone who's got three British kids, a couple of grandchildren and a 35-year-marriage to a Brit is still under threat of losing their rights, then what chance have I got, as a 'Spring chicken' who practically came over yesterday?

Since the Referendum, I've been feeling deeply upset, stressed out, anxious and depressed almost 90% of the time. It seems like the country that I loved so dearly for its tolerance and understanding is no longer here or never really existed!

I've never really regarded myself as an "immigrant", I even find the term offensive. I'm a citizen of the world, above anything else, I just happen to have been born in a different country, so what? I'm mostly upset by my future in-laws' attitude and I honestly feel betrayed. Sure, they've got the right to vote any way they want, and they're not obliged to think about me, but they could have at least thought about their own son! He's happy with me, we've been happy together, and at the age of 50 (soon this year) having to look for another girlfriend in case I can't stay here might not really feel like the best experience in his life, but who cares? As long as they've got "their country back" and the Union Jack is waving proudly all over the place, it's all fine. "You'll be alright" is all they say. My partner thinks so too. He keeps saying there's no way that I will get deported, that he knows his country and how it works and that it'll all be okay.

But should I believe this or face up to reality? I keep hearing of people being refused a PR, even though they've contributed to the British system more than a lot of natives for years. I keep hearing and reading of hate crimes and xenophobic actions. Thankfully I haven't really been subjected to any of that (with very few exceptions that I can't really prove to be based on xenophobia), but I find myself faking my accent as much as possible or lying about my origin, which I've always hated and thought of as pathetic. Whenever asked I lie about my job too, as saying I'm an interpreter is practically admitting to being a non-Brit and I can never be sure if the person chatting to me cheerfully on the train is not a nationalist who would a second later be shouting "BRITAIN FOR THE BRITS!"

So what now?

I really don't know what to do. I'm trying not to make any major decisions quite yet, until I'm absolutely sure what options we've got. I'm currently not eligible for a PR as I haven't lived here for five years and my annual income is below the £18,600 threshold, but I still hope it might turn out not necessary. So far I think we've done what we could. Now it's all a waiting game.

Victoria Nikolova, Bulgaria

★★★

I could not secure a decent job in Spain if I did not speak English. I did not have the money to pay for private tuition so decided to come here to earn money and learn at the same time.

Only two months after arriving here in 2000 I met the Norfolk boy that would become my husband. Within a couple of years it became clear that I was not going back any time soon so I set about carving a future in the UK. I started working for the NHS as a nursing assistant. I took A-levels in the evenings on top of my full time job because I wanted to be able to provide more meaningful help to my patients, a goal that involved going to University. My 11 Spanish A-levels did not count so I took the opportunity to improve my language and writing skills. I was accepted at UEA in 2005, qualifying in 2008. I worked for the NHS throughout my studies, weekends, evenings (A&E x-ray 8pm-1am) and holidays whenever possible on top of my lectures and 1000+ hrs clinical placements.

From graduation I worked in an acute hospital in Norfolk which involved weekend rotas, on-call and two hours commute daily. Some weeks would clock 60+ hours. In 2012, and after trying to get pregnant for over a year (I was 31), I decided that the job was creating too much stress and they decided to cut half of my hours due to 'efficiency savings' so I had to choose between dropping my hours or leaving. I handed my notice and secured an interview within two weeks. However, my new Trust took 11 weeks to get me in post due to HR issues.

I have worked for that Trust since and have had two children in that time and I have almost completed a self-funded MSc while working and raising children, all so I can provide better care for my patients. I was planning to go self-employed last year because I was finding it impossible to do my job to a decent standard within the constraints of funding and current targets. This was until the Brexit vote.

Since June I have had to stay in a job which I hate, within a team full of people who are just trying to survive. I was initially distraught at the change in narrative and for the first time in 16 years I felt not only unwelcome, but that a Britain First attitude was now the way things were going, and as a result I was surplus to requirement and not something to think about. I had to become used to the dismissal of colleagues: "But you are married to a Brit! You will be OK, I do not know what you are worrying about."

I suffered incidents of verbal abuse from patients. Once I was visiting a patient and she seemed to struggle to understand me when I recommended she get a gang plug on a table to avoid having to bend over to the low socket on the wall. Her response floored me: "What are you saying! What are you talking about? Speak proper English for God's sake!" to which I responded that I am Spanish and I was only doing my best. She then went on a rant: "You people come over here and can't even be bothered to learn to speak English properly. This is ridiculous! I will have you know that my husband was an electrician and he would not have it! He would not have had this nonsense! GANG PLUG [really loudly] it is pronounced GANG PLUG! Seriously this is ridiculous!"

Once October came and the Conservative conference unravelled I realised this government was not going to stop the narrative and was actually a source for it, so decided to get the paperwork in place to secure my right to remain. I had been here, working solidly for 16 years, I was married to a Brit, I had two British children and I had contributed to the NHS all this time, I thought it should be fairly straight forward... how mistaken was I proven to be!

Because of university and that three month break in 2012 I was not going to qualify for PR so I decided to do a citizenship application based on the Indefinite Leave to Remain (ILR) I obtained in 2004 in order to attend university (they required it). Even that has not been straightforward and I have had to send 12 years' worth of evidence to prove my right to be here. I am still waiting to hear if I will be given citizenship. Through this I have ended up taking the total of seven week of sickness leave due to anxiety and depression related to work and personal stress. At one point I was frantic and completely helpless due to the lack of clarity and guidance from official bodies and the lack of support from those around us. I continue to struggle and people at work look blank when I try to explain why I feel so vulnerable and helpless. My sense of self-worth continues to be attacked on a daily basis and I need to dig deep to tell myself I am not deserving of this treatment and I do not deserve having everything I have worked so hard for taken away from me.

Sadly though, these difficulties have made me realise this country has had an army of closet xenophobes and nationalists that have succeeded on commanding the narrative, and they have done so mostly unchallenged by those that should be responsible for stamping out this kind of abusive and inhumane behaviour. The damage is done, neither I nor my husband want to raise children in a country so full of hatred and lack of compassion. We are planning to leave. All we have to do is wait for my citizenship so I have the ability to return should his family require us to be here in the future and to secure rights to my pension. We are leaving at great loss to our lives, my career is lost, my husband won't be able to find a job in Spain, we have sold our house, and we will lose our friends and our support network. We face extremely tough times ahead, but that is a worthy sacrifice to get away from a country where we are considered second class citizens.

Olaya, Spain

★★★

I moved to Belfast in the late 80's to study science. Opportunities in Ireland were limited at the time so I stayed in the UK, moving to London to study for my PhD. I have been working in research and as a lecturer since. I am married to a lovely English man who is a professor at a

UK University and we have three school-aged kids. Although I have no issues residing in the UK, I now hate living here. I find the climate since Brexit utterly regressive and insular. I can hardly believe that this country I once thought of as open-minded and outward-looking is hell-bent on a self-destructive path towards small-minded nationalism and protectionism. I am horrified by the xenophobia and racism towards others that I have seen and heard about.

Although I have been contentedly living here and contributing to society for over twenty-five years, I have never really felt very Irish, just European – that was enough. For me, the EU is more important than individual nations; it is where I find my identity and culture. After much soul-searching, heartache (and therapy for me!), we have decided to leave Britain and our lovely network of friends and neighbours, taking our kids out of their schools and head west to Ireland and the EU. My lovely British friends (who largely voted to remain) are puzzled and can't imagine why anyone would choose to leave Britain. A year ago, I would have laughed at this thought, but now I cannot bear the prospect of remaining here. But here we are. The house is on the market, in the summer we will be leaving.

Roisín, Ireland

★★★

23rd June 2016 – the date we have all been dreading for months... Me and my friends, we have already felt a change of attitude towards us in these last few months, and the last few weeks, even more so! We also have heard so many incorrect information and lies being propagated via the media! And the ice on the cake, we can't vote! Our destiny is in someone else's hand... This is so unsettling!

I call my friend after work, we are worried but still hopeful... just a bit anxious! I follow the Referendum on telly... with the children... then later on, on my own... 2am I have gone to bed... I am working in the morning... I get up at 5.30am, woken up by my friend's phone call, crying on the phone! I am stunned... In a way, not surprised. But still in shock! So many feelings and thoughts go through my head! This is a nightmare, am I dreaming?

My son asks me if he would still be allowed to be part of his football team. I tell him not to worry. I drop my children at school and go to work... Everyone is speaking about the news... It's unbearable! Although I don't share my feelings at this point, I just get on with work, supporting our elderly patients to wash, dress, eat, listen to their chit chat, do activities with them... but all I hear from some colleagues, is how happy they are: less of these so called immigrants! I am an immigrant...

Break time, me and a Polish colleague are having a coffee... and in the staff room, there are three people cheering at Brexit; cheering on no more migrants stealing our jobs, cheering on the repatriation of us so called migrants! In any other time, or place, I probably would have butted in, I hate injustice! But this day I just can't cope with it. I'm already devastated. I just want to be around people who understand me, I guess.... my body can't take it anymore... I'm was shaking, I'm sick... I try to stamp on my feelings and get on with work, looking after OUR elderly, trying to be cheerful for them, but I can't... I go home early... I need to offload... I need to scream!

I go home, I go on social media, and start putting a new status. It is my only way to offload: 'My world is crumbling, I can't find the right words to describe how I feel, not just in a selfish way for my sake, and my family's sake, but because of the sad state of affairs, as in people today, even more than these last few months, are really coming out of the underground with racists, vicious, offending comments, and all they talk about is 'foreigners', not about any reasonable or economical basis... sad, sad, sad! I have lived here 17 years, including 12 in Bradford, I love Bradford, but today I do not recognise 'my' town... I feel like an outsider.'

Some of my friends see my status and invite me to uni to offload within a safe space. We have no solution but it helps to talk. In the next few days, British politics seems to be a bit of a blur, something happens daily, resignations, the Leave side accepting they lied all along. It all seems a bit like watching a bad cartoon. What's next?

But also there are more worries for us, as more and more hate incidents arise. I start being wary of even speaking on the phone, or talking in my native language in the street. Even my eldest asks me not to speak French when I pick him up, as he breaks down later on, as some teens told him and his Muslim friend to go back home. My children are born and bred here in the UK, whilst they may be French on paper, they consider themselves British. I start being a bit paranoid... Do people look at me, and only focus in a negative way on me, or my children, being foreigners/ migrants? I am proud to be French, my kids have been brought up to be proud of their French/ Congolese roots whilst integrating fully in the community. Shall we start to hide where we come from?

A few days later, I see people are starting to organise. My friend invites me to be part of a group: 'Bradford says no to racism, Bradford says everyone stays!' This picks up my brain... it will keep my brain busy, and hopeful. Yeah it reminds me it's not totally out of our control, we can organise, we can... 'We'? There's hope! This is the Bradford I know... resilient! We have power to challenge! It's not a 'them vs us' anymore, it's a 'We'... We are Bradfordians together! I get to network, meet new people who accept us, who care about our family, my friends and any other migrants. We, with the kids, get together to do placards with Wur Bradford, we give out leaflets and posters, we create new groups to do petitions to challenge the government not to use us as bargaining chips... We link up with national groups such as the3million, we speak out.

13th July 2016: the day of 'Bradford says no to racism, Bradford says every-one stays', we are a bit anxious still, but as I came with children, friends and family, we are overwhelmed by the love.... the amount of people who came for support (800 people came that day) and even passers-by joining in! The sharing of poetry, stories, music... I love Bradford. The event just gave us a buzz, we just felt so happy, in peace, we felt comfortable at last. Part of Bradford. Proud to be a Bradfordian!

Vie Clerc Lusandu, France

★★★

Here since 2007, good teaching career, many good friends, always thought I'd grow old in this country, fully integrated, feeling strange when going back to Germany on holiday – and then Brexit happened.

On the morning I received a text message from a neighbour, we had been walking together and got on very well. It read: 'We know this news will shock you. But please be certain that we didn't mean you, you will get a visa without problem, we voted against the unchecked immigration that harms the country. We love and cherish you. You will be fine.' These words are still with me nine months later, I don't think I've ever been so offended in my life. I have not spoken to them since.

Like so many I started to manoeuvre in order to protect my assets: applied for PR, my passport was gone for a full five months, very anxious waiting, received my PR in February with the information that I was eligible to apply for citizenship in April. Here is the funny thing: I have no interest in citizenship anymore. None! I have never felt so German and so proud and defensive about it. I'm questioning if I have been lying to myself for the last ten years: are friends my friends? Am I welcome here? Where am I going to end up? Have I wasted my time and energy on this country? Could I make it work back in Germany? To clarify: I'm in no way scared to be deported or even sent away. The shock to my system was more about how things have changed inside of me.

Ultimately, I'm not sure why I'm here anymore, I'm running out of reasons as the days go on. This has not been an easy process: my nightly teeth grinding has increased so much since the summer that I will need surgery for a dislocated disk in my jaw. Wake up call! I can only describe it as a divorce after the beloved partner cheated: the rug has been pulled from under my feet, I feel betrayed, cheated and hurt. I get annoyed with the apparent indifference and political apathy of many of my British friends – we just don't have the same experience anymore. I'm afraid I'm alienating quite a few of them. My family and friends back home don't really understand either. I'm caught between my two cultures with no idea what my next step should be...

Anna K., Germany

★★★

My parents came over from Spain in 1963 to try and create a good and stable life. Things had been very hard in Spain since the Civil War and my father had had to give up on his university course. He would have been a physicist. My mother, the oldest of six, had had to raise her siblings and had no formal education. Things were tough so they came here.

According to my mother, things were strict but fair. They taught themselves English and got jobs in the hospitality industry. My father turned out to be a rather excellent chef de cuisine, with several Michelin accreditations. After four years of working hard and reporting to the police every week, they were given permanent residency and both were over the moon. I was born the following year and their family was complete.

My childhood was a happy one. Parents who worked very hard but who knew how to have fun too. I grew up with the best of both worlds really. We lived in a little village and life was calm. My day was half English (school) and half Spanish (home), and it was great.

Long story short, in all my (almost) 50 years in this country, I have never felt as though my family and I belonged anywhere else. I mean I was born here, my parents integrated so well and they had a lot of friends. There was no reason to believe otherwise. However, since the Referendum I have been publically insulted three times, spat on once and generally looked down upon. All in my own town. I cannot comprehend where all this hatred has come from and why it's being allowed to happen. It seems the xenophobia and general ignorance runs deep and has been buried for a long time. Some now think it's perfectly acceptable to insult those who were once 'friends'.

I am disgusted with what this country is becoming and I am truly ashamed to be British. I am a European citizen and I always will be. I will fight this stupid decision to ruin all our lives until my last breath if necessary.

Cristina Cotillas, UK

★★★

I am German and so is my family. We came to Scotland in August 2003 as we wanted to give our two youngest children the chance to grow up bilingual, and have better chances later in life. My husband is an electrician by trade, and I have a nursing background, but worked the last 10 years in Germany as a manager in a recruitment business.

When we came to the UK, I could not speak English, as I am from a part of Germany (Saarland) where we only had the option to learn French at school. Soon we found out that my husband needed the '16th edition' qualification to legally work as an electrician in the UK, so he went to a training centre to do the course, whilst I took on a job as a home carer (without knowing the language!). I worked 12 hours every day, and my lucky dip was that one of my elderly people used to be an English teacher at a high school. Even though the lady was very ill, and suffered from dementia, she made me sit down at 'tuck in time' every night for 30 minutes, and had me writing first of all words, then sentences, and later on she gave me topics to write a little story about. She then corrected my writings the next day, and even gave me stickers when I was below 10 spelling mistakes. The lady is dead now, but I still have to thank her.

Once my Hubby had his '16th edition', he started to work as an electrician. The girls went to primary school and were fit in the language in no time. In 2005 an opportunity came along, and my husband was offered a job. We moved to a little village in the area. Soon after moving in, we had to face the first attack from locals who told us to go home where we came from. We tried to sort it out, but we discovered soon that some people in the village were really anti-foreigners. Our daughters went to the local primary school, but the kids of the racist family were in their classes, and so there were many small incidents in the following years. When the first of the girls moved on to secondary education, it all started full blast. Name calling, bullying, stolen mobile phone...

In her second year I got a call one morning from one of the girls she was friends with. It soon emerged that my daughter had been beaten up, stamped on her head, her earrings ripped out of her ears, hair pulled out, and a tooth broken. Her mobile was trampled on too and was unusable. I took my daughter to hospital, where she was treated for many injuries, and released the next day. She was signed off for two weeks, and after the two weeks I insisted on her going back, as the police had assured us that it won't happen again, as they wanted to speak to the parents of the girl who'd done it.

Sadly, my daughters were subjected to more harrowing xenophobic bullying and attacks but after we moved again, things calmed down and we all settled back into our lives. That is until the Referendum.

On 24th of June we had to face the music full blast, as people were now openly telling us to go home, before the government will put us on a train with pigs and ship us back to where we came from. On 25th June I went shopping with my younger daughter at a supermarket, and whilst standing at the till, I asked my daughter in German, if we need anything else. A couple at the next till turned their heads around, and said: "They will have to go home too!" My daughter looked at me, and I could see her eyes were filled with tears. I just told her in a firm manner in German that she should swallow the tears for now. I paid, and we both went out with heads high up. We loaded the car, drove away from there, and I had to stop at a quiet stop, because we both could not keep back our tears any more.

Since June we have had at least one or two incidents like this per week. I have been told that soon we will be deported. In hospital I overheard people saying that those foreigners do drain the NHS, when I was there to take my husband after he got his finger in a table saw. People making fun of foreigners and refugees, and even laughing out loud by playing Rule Britannia and talking about Britain belonging to the Brits.

Our son has a British partner, and their children are German-British. We fear for them, as those poor kids might have to go through all this as well. Our son is at the point now, where he thinks about going to Germany with his partner and the kids. The older daughter is in the deepest Highlands, and wants to leave as soon as she has finished her studies. The younger daughter is already in the process of researching places in Europe where she can live and study. So Brexit is in the process of ripping our family apart, because we feel not welcome any more, and I don't want to see my grandkids boarding a pigs-train to somewhere. It hurts, as we have chosen Scotland as our home, and we like where we live.

My husband and me are 50 now, with (at this moment) secure jobs, but we feel we are driven out of this country by xenophobic people and fire fuelling politicians. I have no clue what to do, apart from fighting against Brexit, xenophobia, and ignorance, but it feels like fighting against windmills. Many people try to give us confidence, and tell us that it is only a handful of people who are xenophobic, and that the majority is not like that. Yes, we do hear the words, but they are harder to believe every day. The voices of the haters are getting louder, and louder. The attacks are getting worse. The fear is present 24/7. The trust in people is slowly fading away, and all the colours are fading to grey.

Claudia Karl, Germany

★★★

I met my partner through the skydiving club at the University of Edinburgh almost 20 years ago. After only three months in the city, I fell in love with him, but also the people, the country and EVEN the rain-battered weather (how love affects you in its entirety!). After graduation, we rented a tiny flat in a run-down area of the city, and I found work in a sandwich shop for the first six months, while he worked in a call centre. Oh the glamour! But it was the late 90s, with the Spice Girls encouraging my 'girl power' side to come out, and frankly I loved every minute of it. I looked for a more permanent position while I temped at a university, and soon proved myself to be valuable enough to be invited to apply for a FT job. By that stage, I pretty much decided that I wanted to live with John forever, so wherever he went, I followed! It was a blissful time!

We had visions of a successful career in the UK, followed by a well-earned retirement in France; or maybe Holland (where John's mum came from); or even Germany (after all, I spoke the language pretty well)… or Italy (ah, the nice hills of Tuscany!). Still, it didn't matter what we chose, as for now, we were happy, settled here and had the whole of Europe at our fingertips.

A few years later, he relocated to England and I easily found a new job at a university, as I would not consider not working. I believe in being active, working and contributing to society and generally doing my best to not be 'a burden'. Fast forward a further 12 years, and I'm in a new job (still in

HE) and with a house we now own. With plans of expansions, we decided last year to spend quite a lot of money on renovating and selling, in the hope we'd find a bigger, better house nearby.

The morning of the result, John woke me up saying, 'We're out.' The night before, I joked to my colleagues that I may not be in at work if the Leave vote won, as I'd have packed my bags already (John also mocked my suggestion and said, "Shall I be with the runaway car outside your office tonight?") Those three little words completely shook my world. I kept repeating, "Oh my God, I can't believe it…" many, many times. I went to work in a stupor, and quite teary. What would become of me then? Did 'they' not want me here anymore? Would we need to leave the country as soon as possible? What if we couldn't secure a job elsewhere? Would we have to live separately at first until John could join me in France? Surely, they couldn't legally ask me to leave after all this time? Would I have to live with my parents again in the meantime? Would we be able to support ourselves?

All these irrational questions twirled around in my head, and it was even more of a surprise, when on arrival at work, several members of staff clamoured, "Yeah! Finally, out!! SEE, not all people who voted out are uneducated idiots!" What I wanted to shout back was "SHUT UP! Can't you see you're talking about ME going out too?" I even said back to someone next to me "Well, that's me going. I hate how I feel today, "to which she replied, "Oh don't worry, you'll be fine." I said "Yeah, probably," (trying to convince myself too).

In the next few days and weeks, the excited words of theirs kept twirling in my mind 'so, she and he voted 'out'; they are the ones who don't want me here'. I knew it wasn't rational, but couldn't help but felt betrayed and at opposite ends of the emotional spectrum from how elated they felt. I am not like them, I am now 'the other'. The one that was not born here; the one that will from now on forever be 'the odd one', the 'European oddity we no longer want anything to do with'.

I've always felt pretty much 'part of the furniture', never been discriminated against or made to feel different. Sure, people have commented on my 'accent', but it's always been in complimentary terms and prior to Brexit, I felt quite proud to own a 'sexy' twang. Since last June however, the distance between me (French citizen) and them (UK citizens) has felt like a chasm. It's not just 'where I come from' now, but 'where I should go next'. I never truly questioned what could become of me outside the UK (it would have been my choice, what I would have preferred, at a point in time of my choosing). Now however, I have to review everything (and uprooting after 20 years is not a small feat). I have never worked outside of the UK, I have bought property here, I have built a sizeable pension fund, I have a TV license, a great many pieces of furniture, a contract with a gas company and a subscription to a magazine! That's not even talking about connections made along the years (many good friends, met throughout the years lived here, via various hobbies and work). So, all this would be lost? What if I had to live abroad? Should I come and visit as a 'tourist' in future and pine for the old life that I had and chose NOT to leave, but was compelled to? That sounds risible!

On the other hand, the prospect of having to produce copious documents to prove I've been here for what feels like forever seems equally ridiculous. Just look into it for a minute, and you'll find the answer! Surely, someone, somewhere could prove to you I've been working for 20 years without having to disburse a £65 fee for the privilege?! I am not an 'alien' in a country where I don't belong. I am legally entitled to stay and it hurt my feelings (and my wallet) that you are asking me to justify myself. (When I say 'you', I'm not even sure who it is I have to answer to. Brexiteers? Theresa May? The government?) I know a great number of people feel ashamed that I should go through the wringer and do tell me I am a valued member of UK society. However, for every ten of those, one negative comment or article read in the news offsets that feeling of being welcome and wanted.

How do I feel today? Well, having gone through the 'cycle of grief' like many other EU citizens, I feel I am slowly reaching the bargaining stage (i.e., after all this, could I possibly live elsewhere? I'll have to I guess!) I have spent days and sometimes weeks in a state of anger, then denial and throughout winter was most definitely going through a depressive state. I have felt so low that my husband was concerned for my well-being. I have had 'mysterious ailments' (none of them serious, but diagnosed as stress-induced. I was told to 'take it easy'. Easier said than done!)

It is affecting how I feel about my life here, and although I feel I am giving up the fight, I fear this government has managed to wear me out. It will be another year possibly until I find my feet elsewhere, but they have managed to knock the wind off my sails. I cannot see myself reaching the 'accepting stage'. The situation has forever marred my feelings towards the country and since the Referendum, the constant rhetoric that if we feel European we are 'citizens of nowhere' has made me feel I no longer belong here. My feelings, convictions and political affiliations are at odd with what goes on currently. Everything seems to point out to a narrower, navel gazing country I do not feel comfortable living in. The open, multicultural and cosmopolitan Britain of yesterday that attracted me so much has become 'little England' with all its xenophobia and pettiness high-lighted and revealed at its vilest.

As I write this, I can hear the jibes (read across the social media world) of 'goodbye, don't let the door hit you on your way out' and 'good riddance'. 'You snowflakes just want to draw attention to yourselves when there is no need. Nobody will be evicted, come on, that stands to reason'. However, 'reason' has been missing for many months now. How can I rest easy when every day brings a list of nonsensical decisions, and ever increasingly worrying (and ludicrous) headlines? Even if it is an irrational fear, or even if I am not specifically 'at risk of eviction', I am feeling it in all its unpleasantness and please do not dare tell me how I should feel or not to be hurt. I no longer wish to live here if I am not wholly accepted for who I am. I have not chosen to be born elsewhere, but I thought that by choosing this country, it would 'repay' me for my loyalty and contribution. How wrong I was!

Carole Berreur, France

★★★

Dear Son,

Often I wonder how I'm gonna tell you, why we can't stay in your home. Why you are not gonna sleep in your bedroom that we painted and decorated for hours and hours. Why you won't be able to pop over to your beloved Granny's anymore.

I know that I will have to do the dirty job even though this is not my choice. This will break your heart. For the moment you're still too young but in two years' time. You will ask...

I will have to explain to you that the same people who came to your first birthday party in May, voted for us to LEAVE the country in June. That this sweet 'auntie' who offered you a bicycle that day, made fun of me and laughed when I explained to her how much this will hurt our family. Or will I ever tell you that your closest uncle's reactions to my fears and frustrations, was to tell me to fuck off back to France and that basically he couldn't care less about your rights as a EU citizen? Except your Granny, they ALL voted to leave. And since our lives have been thrown in turmoil.

I love you with all my heart and always will put your interest first. I hope some kind of agreement will be found for helping us to go to France (because if we were made to leave tomorrow we would be homeless). I have nightmares of people taking me away from you: this would simply kill me. We are between a rock and a hard place, just remember everything in life is temporary even our deepest sorrow.

I don't know when, how or where but Son I promise you that we will be fine.

Sophie Ferrand, France

BRITS ABROAD

British citizens in the EU

As I have lived in Cyprus for 25 years, I was unable to vote in the Referendum, which left me with intense feelings of frustration, regret and concern. I have two children, who are both British and Cypriot, and their futures have been affected by the Brexit decision, as has my own. I have always brought them up with a European outlook, with firm roots in the UK, through regular visits home. One will begin his studies at university in September, and the second one now has an uncertain future as he is due to come to study in 2018 (after serving his military service in Cyprus) and the university fee status has yet to be decided or confirmed leading to uncertainty and anxiety.

In my capacity as Deputy Headmistress of an English curriculum international school in Cyprus for several years, I have assisted over 1500 EU students in applying for higher education in the UK. While in the UK, I believe that these students, in addition to the obvious economic benefit to the UK, have offered an invaluable contribution through their skills and culture. I am a firm believer in education promoting tolerance and awareness and am greatly concerned that this will be adversely affected if European students are affected by the Brexit and no longer able to come to the UK to study. Their interaction with UK students is paramount in preventing UK students from becoming isolated and insular in their outlook. After all, the essence of higher education is international by nature and Brexit-style restrictions on movements across borders will not serve this purpose. The increase in post-Brexit hate-crime is absolutely alarming.

Many of our students are now working in the UK (as EU citizens) and have fabulous careers in professions such as engineering and designing the new Crossrail system in London or in leading banks and firms. Not to mention those who dedicate their lives to the NHS as doctors. These young people are deeply disappointed and demoralised currently.

As an 'outsider' (which I am now made to feel) looking at what is happening in the UK from a distance, I am appalled at the lack of apparent answers relating to this momentous decision. I am highly embarrassed when I answer the many daily calls I receive from anxious Cypriot parents about their children's future studies in the UK – all I can say is, "I don't know," or "It has not been confirmed." Many of these families have made great sacrifices (and of course planned many years ahead) to ensure that their children can have a top-rate UK education as it has always been held in the highest regard in Cyprus. I too have played a role in promoting this.

It is with great disappointment and sadness that I watch the TV updates daily, seeing how many people running campaigns have lied (and proved to be British 'quitters') and this has had a dire effect on so many lives, a fact they now seem to take no responsibility for.

I feel greatly let down by my home country and deeply embarrassed and ashamed by the presentation of the UK abroad as being a country that is without leadership and without concrete plans and answers. Great Britain has always been a country that has been admired for its economic strength, organisation and efficiency. This image has now been irreparably damaged and no-one takes responsibility.

Kam Stylianou, UK citizen living in Cyprus

★★★

As an Englishman living in Germany and denied a vote, my perspective is different to that of the Europeans in the UK, but we share similarities all the same. It's only since I've been abroad (and particularly since the dreadful vote of June 23rd) that I have come to fully appreciate just how I was subject to the drip, drip, drip brainwashing as a child and growing up in England. We were the British, victors of WW2 and by default better than everyone else. It was the Great Escape and the Dambusters every holiday on TV. I even read war comics like Victor and Commando where the Germans were the square-jawed aliens uttering robotic sayings like "Achtung, Achtung" and "Surrender, Englischer Schweinhund!" Everything we did had to be slightly different – drive on the left, imperial weights and measures, even 'Jeux Sans Frontières' on TV couldn't be translated literally (it had to be called 'It's a Knockout!' – which made no sense at all).

'The Continent' was somewhere away across the water, full of people who were inherently inferior somehow, even if it wasn't expressed directly in those terms.

Somehow, I managed to ditch most of this nonsense baggage I'd been saddled with. Marrying a German and experiencing other Europeans first-hand has taught me the truth of the situation. Empire days are long gone. We need Europe. Forty years of progress are now being thrown away. My sister and my best friend in the UK voted Leave. I don't recognise the country anymore and don't want to be associated with it now. I hate what this ridiculous Referendum has done to my country and my relationship with people who are close to me. I truly believe that future generations will condemn this period in our history in the same way that we now look back at the madness of the First World War.

G. Bower, UK citizen living in Germany

★★★

In 2002, with a bit of a career and 2.2 kids in tow, my wife and I decided it would be a good thing if I accepted a job at a bank in Brussels. Partly because it would mean a better life-work balance (I was freelancing), but also because we thought it would be a better environment for the kids, and would avoid having to commit to one of the fairly glum school choices at home. We liked the idea of public transport that you could rely on, healthcare with choice, and Brussels is easy to get to from home. The bank didn't work out, but I went freelance again, eventually propping up the IT department at one of the EU institutions.

These rights to free movement are very real to us. We pay more taxes here, but we've had great healthcare, family allowance currently covers university costs, the tax regime hasn't changed significantly, and the environment is very positive towards freelancers (if IR35 means something to you, enough said).

So 15 years later, we now find ourselves faced with total uncertainty about those rights. A hard Brexit with the loss of pension and healthcare rights and having to pay non-EU university rates would cost us as a family something in the region of three to six years' income. We don't even know if we could move back to the UK in case of retirement, ill health or other unforeseen circumstances, as we're currently entrenched in the Belgian social security system.

The default assumption about the British has been that you are someone very creative with a fresh way of thinking who can bring a lot to a Belgian or international environment. Not anymore. People here have come to understand post-Brexit Britain as a country riddled with problems, poor government, lousy language skills, an unbalanced economy, and worst of all, hatred. I'm pleased that I saw both sides and could bring my kids up on the side I chose.

So that's my story. My right to leave is being thrown away by people who have no understanding how valuable that right is.

Jeremy Thomas, UK citizen living in Belgium

HOPE

Well two strange things happened to us. My French husband, JC, had been asked by a work colleague, the day after the Referendum, when he was leaving. A couple of days ago, this colleague approached JC and said that he had only been joking, that as JC was married to a Brit, he had nothing to worry about. Well JC put him in the picture – a very complete picture of what it means to the three million, what has been happening, the implications regardless of being married to a Brit etc. The colleague listened carefully and not only apologised, not only did he admit he had been in the wrong, but he went as far as saying, given the chance again, he would vote to Remain.

Then there was me and my workplace. Every one of my colleagues, I am pleased to say, voted to remain – apart from one. He was very vociferous during the campaigning with his arguments to leave, and when the results came through, he was as pleased as punch and called us all 'losers'. Today was his last day at work – he is moving on to pastures new, and as rarely happens, we had our break at the same time. He brought up politics and I thought, well it is his last day, I will debate with him, not avoid the subject – after all he won't be on my case much longer. The subject quickly came around to Brexit and he asked whether JC had become a British citizen. I explained the case in great detail – expecting an argument – but no he was astounded, and suggested that "those people who voted for Brexit based it on rubbish in the newspapers and on the side of a bus." He went on to suggest that the EU was a good thing for us – pointing out projects that had been financed by the EU, the laws that protected our employment rights. He went on and on. I didn't say a word about him changing his tune – I wondered whether he thought I might have forgotten his Brexiteering and boasting about being on the winning side.

JC had his Brexit regretter, but me I got myself a Brexit denier. A bit too late, I know, but despite the fact it changes nothing for us all, I had a little bit of a feeling of hope.

Joanne Gollandeau, UK

★★★

I'm Polish. I came to Northern Ireland for the first time in 2003 as an Erasmus student. I stayed for half a year, went home to finish my degree, then came back again to do a PhD and – as it later turned out – to stay permanently.

Some people may think that there is nothing holding me here. I haven't started a family, and I haven't got a mortgage. I'm not even doing professional research anymore. Even before I finished my PhD, I had already understood that I was not going to particularly like the challenges of the academic work and lifestyle. And so it is: I rent my house, I avoid dating, and I earn pennies as a university librarian. Not an easy or especially fulfilling life, you might say, but I see it differently.

I am very happy here. The people are kind; the weather is mild; and the landscape is so beautiful that I couldn't change it for the world. I love my job. It is the best job ever for a bookworm. I love my friends, 'made in wine but proven in tears'. After 12 years of living here, I can't even survive long without a decent amount of rain. I literally dry up every time I visit Poland.

Even though I have quit academic research, I've never lost interest in what I came to study in the first place. I specialise in Irish medieval history, and I still do plenty of work in this area, even though it is no longer strictly academic. I am writing a novel inspired by my past research, and it is a wonderful adventure, enriching my life intellectually as well as emotionally. In other, much shorter, words: I love this place, and I don't intend to leave it.

Northern Ireland voted Remain, and, as a foreigner, I can really feel it. I've heard all kinds of awful stories from and about the immigrants living in England – the harsh words addressed to them, the cases of verbal or physical aggression, the disgusting leaflets put through their doors – but here it feels different. Of course, I do understand that there are no places in the world that are perfectly free of fear, aggression, or prejudice. We do hear about unpleasant incidents happening here, too, but they are very rare, and they are widely and overwhelmingly condemned. Northern Irish people are probably no better or worse than any other people anywhere in the world, but they do have it fresh in their memory what hate speech and prejudice may lead to, and they are doing their best to prevent that from happening again.

Dr Judyta Szacitło, Poland

OUR BREXIT BLOG

Please keep on reading, on our blog http://www.ourbrexitblog.eu/, more of our compelling testimonies by:

A.M., Italy
Aga B., Poland
A.K., UK
Anonymous, France
Anonymous, Germany
Anonymous, Poland
Anonymous, UK
Anonymous, Europe
A.P.M., UK
Benjamin Schwarz, UK
C., Europe
Caroline, UK
Elke, Belgium
EU citizen of Germany
Gabriella, Hungary
H. S. Norway
Ingrid, Denmark
Judit Kertesz-Gruber, Hungary
Juliet Sen-Gupta, UK
K.K., Germany
Magdalena Sminiarska, Poland
Marta Pacholec, Poland
Meike Brunkhorst, Germany
M.S., Portugal
Natalia, Spain
O.P., dual citizen of Canada & Italy
Peter, The Netherlands

Sarah (and the rest of the family), UK
Simona, Romania
Susi, Austria
Symon Silvester, UK
Yasmin, UK/Spain
Dr Wouter Servaas, The Netherlands

And feel free to add your voice to ours.

Our Blog: www.OurBrexitBlog.eu
Our Email: OurBrexitTestimonies@gmail.com
Our FB Page: www.facebook.com/OurBrexitTestimonies
Our Twitter: @OurBrexitTesti

THANK YOU!

The making of this book would not have been possible without the help and support of some very special people.

Our most sincere gratitude goes to…

George Szirtes for his moving and beautiful foreword.
Gareth Harrey for his book cover that expresses so well what our book is about and for the book design.
Frank Machalowski for his forest photo used in the cover design.

And to our dedicated team of moderators/administrators

Anne-Laure Donskoy, Admin
Adda Macchich, blog/moderator
Cosi Doerfel Hill, moderator
Dr Helen De Cruz, moderator
Saskia Slottje, moderator
Nathalie Clarke, moderator
Laura Sironi, moderator
Patrizia Mayall, moderator

Miles Martin, organisation/logistics
Alessandro Martinez, organisation/logistics

Thanks also to our friends:

Nicolas Hatton, co-chair of the3million
Drs Mike Galsworthy & Rob Davison, co-directors Scientists for EU
Prof. Emmy van Deurzen
Vittorio Quattrone, Europeans

Kristina Strömberg, EU Citizens IN The UK And British EU Citizens Abroad
Claudia Borgognoni Holmes, UK citizenship EU nationals, UKCEN
Sarah Parker, "Campaign for Europe"
I LOVE MY 'FOREIGN' SPOUSE': defend the rights of cross-border couples
The 48%

A big thank you too to all those who have supported this publication and in particular:

Charlotte Morrow
Manuel Ignacio Fernandez Orellana
Lap Ging Leong
Elly Wright
Pascale Rigley
Silvia De Martini
Monique Hawkins
Silvana Parsons
Jonathan Sweet
Anny Robin
Sarah Pybus
Mari Turnbull
Laure Om
Laura Sironi
Francesco and Luisa Armezzani
Cristina Saponaro
Anne David
Marina Signoretto
Lisa Stagg
Vie Clerc Lusandu
Silvana Lanzetta
Lora Noncheva-Tabakova
And many more...

And to those who have helped us by sharing the crowdfunding page:

Monique Hawkins
Francesca Morosini
Laure O.M.
Kam Stylianou
Sumi Olson
Rosa Weisener
Murielle Stentzel
Nadia Söderman
Beatrice Kindred

And, finally, a massive thank you to all the wonderful people who have trusted us with their testimonies. May this collective book of ours touch hearts and open minds!

Elena and Véronique

18384011R00149

Printed in Poland
by Amazon Fulfillment
Poland Sp. z o.o., Wrocław